Trees and buildi

Trees and buildings

Complement or conflict?

Edited by Tony Aldous

This publication is based on the proceedings
of a conference organised by
The Tree Council and the Royal Institute of British Architects
and held at the RIBA, 66 Portland Place, London W1
on 7 March 1979

The Landscape Institute, The Royal Institution of Chartered Surveyors
and The Royal Town Planning Institute were also associated with the
conference.

RIBA Publications Limited and The Tree Council

Photographic credits

Countryside Commission 7.1 to 7.5
de Burgh Galwey 8.4 (Courtesy *Architectural Review*)
Malcolm Griffiths 6.1, 6.2
Archie Handford 8.5
Owen Lawrence 5.7
A. E. Mc R. Pearce 8.2, 8.3
M. D. Trace 1.1 to 1.6
Colin Westwood 5.1, 5.3, 5.4, 5.5
Brian Williams 6.5, 6.6
All other photos by individual contributors.

© Copyright RIBA Publications Limited 1979 and all individual contributors

Published jointly by RIBA Publications Limited, Finsbury Mission, Moreland Street, London EC1V 8VB and The Tree Council, 33 Belgrave Square, London SW1X 8QN

ISBN: 0 900 630 73 6
Printed in Great Britain.

Contents

Page 7		Foreword: Andrew Breach
9	1	Introduction: Tony Aldous
13	2	A surveyor's view: Jack D. Campling
23	3	Problems of proximity: Dr Evan R.C. Reynolds
31	4	Practical tests and conclusions: Dr P. Giles Biddle
40	5	Keeping and planting trees on development sites: Ivor Cunningham
47	6	Planting trees on bare housing sites: R. Neil Higson
54	7	Trees in the wider landscape: Paul N. Walshe
67	8	A countryman's view: John Weller
75	9	The green people; a Dutch view: Ir. Jan L. Guldemond
84	10	Trees in the inner city: Ian White
93		Glossary
94		Bibliography

Foreword

Andrew Breach, Chairman, Bristol & West Building Society

I sometimes wonder whether, both as private individuals and as busy professional men and women, we are not subjected to rather more advice than is good for us; too many reports, too many consultative documents and too many official recommendations. Of course, the problem is often compounded by media coverage which inevitably simplifies the issues by ironing flat the 'ifs' and 'buts' which provide the crucial perspective.

These thoughts are prompted by a recollection of the alarm caused last year by the content of the draft British Standard on tree planting near buildings. That document has since been modified but in its original form it seemed, as Tony Aldous puts it, to be a blueprint for tree-less towns and suburbs. This was a threat serious enough to inspire the initiative of a number of bodies, notably the Tree Council and the Royal Institute of British Architects, to combine in staging a conference earlier this year at which the issues could be properly discussed.

What emerged from that conference was the need for a sense of proportion (in both the pro- and anti-tree lobbies), a recognition that some trees, in certain circumstances and on certain sites *can* cause structural problems, but that the risks — highlighted by two successive summers of drought — had in some respects been exaggerated. Above all, the need for further research was widely recognised. I welcome this book, which should help to open up the debate to a wider audience.

We need many more, not fewer, trees, although trees in towns should not, it seems to me, be perceived as substitutes for good looking houses, offices or factories; their function is not to hide ugly buildings but to soften, enrich and 'humanise' our living and working surroundings. But if we need trees, they also need us. They need friends, and good friends who can recognise that they do have faults as well as virtues. This is why I believe that this book will help safeguard their future in our cities and towns.

1 Introduction

Tony Aldous

Tony Aldous is a freelance environmental and architectural journalist. Formerly environment and architectural Reporter of *The Times*, he is now consultant to the Civic Trust, consultant editor of the monthly *Rehab* supplement of *Building* magazine, and writes regularly for *Illustrated London News* and *The Countryman*.

During the two exceptionally dry summers and the intervening dry winter of 1975-76, many houses and other buildings suffered damage as a result of the drying out of soil under and around their foundations. This damage was more extensive and serious on certain kinds of soil, notably the so-called 'shrinkable clays' which occur in such areas as south east Essex. Surveyors' reports often connected this damage with nearby trees; and in a large number of cases trees did at least contribute to the trouble. This is because, as Dr Evan Reynolds explains in Chapter 3, a tree's root system effectively forms an underground extension of the soil's evaporating surface.

But in that alarming aftermath of the 1975-76 drought, the role of trees in damaging buildings came to be much exaggerated. A little learning was indeed a dangerous thing. Laymen, and even professionals, who should have known better, indulged in sweeping generalisations and over-simplifications. These ignored not only the widely different capacities of different soils to shrink and 'heave' (ie, expand), but the divergent characteristics of the root systems of different tree species, and the different resilience of different forms of construction. It was almost as if, needing a scapegoat — or, at least, needing a simple explanation for a complex phenomenon difficult to understand, let alone explain — they turned as a man on the one visible and defenceless individual palpably still remaining at the scene of the crime: the tree.

There are, in fact, as structural surveyor Jack Campling makes clear in Chapter 2, particular reasons apart from the Great Drought why surveyors and others should have been casting about for scapegoats and requiring expensive (and often unnecessary) remedial work to damaged buildings. These have to do with the decision of insurance companies in 1972 for the first time to include subsidence of foundations as a risk generally covered in their policies. With hindsight, one can see that the effect on people's attitudes was inevitable. Where the ordinary householder carries that risk himself, as he did before 1972, he will tend to carry out only such remedial

Introduction: Aldous

1.1 and 1.2
St Clement Danes, Strand, London
With trees (actual) and (by photographic sleight of hand) without trees.

work as is essential — he will plaster over superficial cracks and hope (usually quite justifiably) that a resumption of normality in the British climate will fill up the water table and put an end to his worries. But if his own or his neighbour's insurance company is paying, he wants the full treatment: he wants a guaranteed remedy, or as near to a guaranteed remedy as the professionals can devise. After all, that is what we pay insurance companies for — to let us sleep quiet o' nights.

So the professionals and technicians devised ingenious, expensive, and frequently quite unnecessary remedies to damage caused by soil shrinkage. And the more expensive the remedies became, the more necessary it seemed to have a scapegoat. Moreover, as two of our contributors point out, this society of ours has its share of 'tree-haters', an 'anti-tree lobby'. If we seek to explain this phenomenon more rationally, or at least more charitably, we may infer that these are people who for one reason or another weigh the disadvantages of trees (damage from roots, loss of light, leaves blocking gutters, and so on) much more heavily in the balance than they weigh their aesthetic and ecological advantages.

This anti-tree lobby found a peg to hang its propaganda on with the circulation in 1978 of a draft British Standard for the planting of trees near buildings. This document has since been withdrawn and substantially rewritten by a working party chaired by Mr Hal Moggridge, partner to Sylvia Crowe and now President of the Landscape Institute, so it seems pointless to (so to speak) rake over those particular dead leaves. Suffice to say that the original draft was in some respects excessively cautious in its advice as to how close you could plant various species to buildings in various soils; and that, inevitably, publicity about the draft (and those who precipitately sought to act upon it) tended to miss the crucial small print of reservation and exception. Now to comply with the conditions of the National House-Building Council for its guarantees to house-buyers, a builder must generally follow BSI standards; and without a

Introduction: Aldous

NHBC certificate, a housebuyer will have difficulty in getting a mortgage. The British Standard on trees and buildings was therefore crucial. Adoption (and misapplication) of the original draft seemed, in the kind of tight-packed urban development we mostly have today, to be a recipe for treeless towns and suburbs in the future.

So the 'tree people' — or 'green people', as our Dutch contributor Jan Guldemond would call them — rose in revolt. Their counter-attack centred on persuading the British Standards Institution to take back and re-write its draft text; and it also included a joint initiative by the Tree Council, the Royal Institute of British Architects, the Royal Institution of Chartered Surveyors, and the Landscape Institute (the professional body for landscape architects, managers and scientists) to mount a conference on the subject. That conference, which took place at the RIBA's headquarters in London on 7 March 1979, was hugely over-subscribed. The list of its 400 participants included not only architects, landscape architects, foresters and arboriculturalists, but also local authority planners concerned with development control and conservation, engineers, surveyors, builders, and even property developers. It demonstrated clearly a great public interest and thirst for information on the subject.

This response encouraged the RIBA and the Tree Council not only to contemplate further conferences elsewhere in Britain, but to distill the valuable advice and information contained in the conference papers into this book. Some of the contributors, like Dr Evan Reynolds, Dr Giles Biddle, and Essex surveyor Jack Campling, deal very much with the nitty-gritty of interaction between trees and buildings. Others, such as landscape architects Neil Higson and Ian White, are more concerned to demonstrate the inestimable gains to the living and working environment that can be, and have been, achieved by tree-planting and well-designed landscape schemes; and to show, that with care and knowledge, the physical risk to buildings need be no more than minimal. Trees are not the

1.3 and 1.4
St Pauls, Covent Garden, London
With and without trees.

1   Introduction: Aldous

villains they are painted. A third group of contributors ranges more broadly over the whole field of landscape design and care, hammering home the point that, whether in town or countryside, trees and attractively treed landscapes do not just happen. They need to be thought out, striven for, and then continuously cared for, managed, and renewed.

In the foyer of the RIBA's Florence Hall on the day of the conference, the Tree Council displayed a series of dramatic 'before and after' photographs: familiar London scenes as they are now (with trees) and — by photographic sleight of hand — as they would be were the trees removed. Those photographs, (1.1 to 1.6) reproduced alongside this introduction, underline the truth that we take trees for granted. We tend to notice them only when they cause trouble or, paradoxically, when threatened with their removal. Yet, I repeat, *trees do not just happen.* Landscape architects can these days, it is true, in exceptional circumstances and at a price, produce 'instant landscape', importing semi-mature trees to soften and adorn hard-edged urban landscapes. But generally speaking trees need time, sustained care, and understanding.

Contrary to the dire prognostications of the 'anti-tree lobby', trees and buildings are not natural enemies. They are complementary elements in a civilised environment. To enable them to live agreeably together, we need, *not* draconian edicts pronouncing their banishment or precipitate execution, but greater knowledge, understanding, forethought, and care.

1.5 and 1.6
Tottenham Court Road (West), London
With and without trees.

2 A surveyor's view

J.D. Campling

Jack Campling, FRICS, FArb, is senior director, building surveying, in the Southend estates and surveying practice, Bairstow Eves. From 1960 to 1975 he acted primarily as a structural surveyor especially for property in the south Essex belt of highly shrinkable clays. A member of the Royal Institution of Chartered Surveyors' working party on Contract Administration, he now administers his company's staff of building surveyors. He lives in a self-designed house at Thorpe Bay, Essex, significantly sited on a patch of non-shrinkable brick earth, and chosen also for its mature trees.

My main connection with this subject is that I have practised for many years in the home counties and particularly in that fruitful nursery for subsidence claims, south east Essex, and have undertaken several thousand investigations of mostly residential properties for potential purchasers and owners. I have, therefore an extensive experience of the outcome of the labours of others and in many cases, of the serious social and economic consequences for those who are judged liable, be they architect, engineer, surveyor, insurance company or lay householder.

Most of this contribution stems from remarks made in the introduction to the several different speakers and subjects dealt with in the first half of the Conference and consequently, is not intended to be comprehensive or profound.

In the context of this book they do, however, have some relevance as in my view the real problem is not so much the technical difficulty, which society has been happy to live with for many thousands of years, but the changing standards and expectations of society itself, as expressed by the Law, its interpretation and the nature of reporting by the media.

It often falls to me as a structural surveyor, to be the first to recognise the seriousness of defects in existing buildings and also then, to impart this intelligence to the owner. This may be by direct advice or more commonly by a potential purchaser withdrawing from his acquisition with the remark 'The surveyor has turned it down' or 'I have had a bad survey report'.

I can assure you that in most cases, such remarks are euphemisms for 'My wife doesn't like the colour of the kitchen' or 'We have been fighting like tigers for a week as she wants to live near her mother – over my dead body!'

Nevertheless, many defects do occur in structures and most should not arise for in each and every case, buildings are designed by one individual or team with expertise, are built by another, are supervised by another, are checked and overseen by others in the form of statutory and quasi-statutory authorities and all these participants in the building process, assert that they are trained and experienced professionals. It is unfortunately a myth that defects arise only from the work of the unqualified, the untrained and the unscrupulous.

'Trees never *cause* **problems . . .'**

Coming to an existing building after all these trained individuals have been involved, the surveyor should only have to be looking for the effects of neglect or misguided amateur activity. Undoubtedly, some surveyors over-emphasise matters that may not be considered by all to be of serious importance or are over cautious, but any surveyor with any significant experience has far too many cases of serious defects which have been designed into or built into buildings with the predictable result that there will be a requirement at best, for excessive maintenance and at worst for major structural repair during the prime period of its life. In most of these cases, the cause and effect could and should have been anticipated and avoided.

We are resolved to consider the relationship between buildings and trees. With new buildings, trees never *cause* problems. They are merely one of many factors which must be allowed for in design and construction. If damage occurs, it is the fault of the designer not of the tree, although the Law takes a different view. With existing buildings, new plantings do develop to create conditions which could not be anticipated by the designer or the builders.

Few people in this country would be happy with an environment without trees, and of course, they have always been with us and have always caused buildings to move. One effect of the proximity of trees on buildings is physical growth, damaging drains or cables and comparatively rarely, the buildings themselves. Probably in total most damage is caused simply by leaves blocking gutters and drains; but when structural problems do arise, it is usually from the effect of tree roots upon the soil upon which the building rests, particularly in clays which change bulk as their moisture content varies.

'Advised to sit tight'

Before the 1939-45 War, the practice was that you just did not use a site for building until it had been cleared of trees and had been left fallow for ten years. It was not explained why, it was just accepted that that was what was done. With the pressure upon building land over the last twenty five years, increasingly suspect sites have been developed and yet more buildings are built closer and closer to site boundaries with their mature trees or on land too recently cleared of natural growths. Prior to 1972, however, moderate seasonal clay distortion, whether caused by trees or not, was usually dealt with by advice to the owner to sit tight, do nothing until recovery had occurred, and then make good with cosmetic repairs.

In my working lifetime, seriously dry seasons have occurred approximately once every seven years and when the normal winter followed with its usual rainfall, clays which had shrunk during the summer, expanded and the buildings returned effectively to their previous state. In some areas, up to 90% of pre-1935 buildings have 'subsided' regularly to one degree or another yet they were subsequently repeatedly bought and sold, accepted as mortgage securities and taken on insurance without difficulty.

'Somebody must be made to pay'

Since 1972, the situation has changed dramatically for two fundamental reasons:

1. The major insurance companies who provide block cover to the borrowers of the principal building societies were pressured to reduce premiums; but rather than do this, they gratuitously increased the cover offered to include 'subsidence and landslip of the site'. Previously subsidence insurance could not be obtained for ordinary domestic properties at any price.

2. The advent and extension of consumer protection legislation without the support of the media has, rightly or wrongly, induced in the minds of many that they live or ought to live in a society where, if anything at all goes wrong, it must be made perfect and somebody must be held to blame and made to pay.

One practical effect of this combination of circumstances and in my view, a most important problem of proximity, is that the unprecedented sequence of dry winters and summers culminating in the summer of 1976, led to such enormous costs not only to the insurance companies but particularly for thousands of individual house owners and occupiers. These householders have not only had to contribute towards extensive underpinning and structural repairs, plus substantial increases in premium costs, but in many cases and this has been the most distressing factor, have had their family, social and psychological world turned upside down by consequences beyond their control and understanding.

'Severe psychological stress'

My own files refer to literally dozens of ordinary people including the terminally sick, widows, single parents, confused elderly people, proud housewives and many others who have suffered severe psychological stress for up to two years over a problem which in the majority of cases, would have been dismissed as a passing inconvenience at any time in our history, prior to 1972. This shows all too plainly that a considered professional opinion, a public or private policy, or a commercial judgement prepared with the best intentions, can sometimes rebound to the serious disadvantage of people least able to cope with it.

It is my own view as a surveyor that any new structure or building should be designed and built to the highest standards and that it is neither practical nor desirable for those standards to be lowered.

It therefore follows that any existing condition within or under the site, in the interaction between different methods of construction or materials, or in the ability of specified elements to satisfactorily perform their function, which could have been anticipated by the professions and the industry, must be accepted by them as their responsibility when failures occur.

It is, however, in considering the existing housing stock where such high minded idealistic approaches to remedial works are believed to be totally unjustified in many cases, when judged by the advantages achieved against the cost and the degree of disturbance suffered by owners and occupiers.

Bottomless pit

There does seem to be a general assumption by many, that in dealing with any structural defect covered by insurance, whether directly under the 'household comprehensive subsidence and landslip' cover of a domestic policy or by way of a claim against the negligence policy of professional adviser or the unfortunate adjoining owner of an offending tree, the allegedly bottomless pit of the insurance industry makes it unnecessary to consider the cost/advantage ratio of remedial works to the same degree as if the owner of the damaged building had to fund repairs from his own resources.

However in the medium term, insurance companies do not lose money. At the end of the day, it is the consumer who pays as for everything else — and 'consumer' includes a high proportion of individuals on a fixed or low income, whose number is likely to increase whilst the present trend for wider home ownership continues.

Isolated trial holes

In judging the real cause of subsidence, brought about by soil contraction or the opposite effect, heave, caused by subsoil expansion, a great deal of factual knowledge of the nature of the subsoil and the actual disposition, type and extraction potential of roots is required. One or two isolated trial holes, often situated in positions of maximum damage rather than of maximum causation, are only a vague general indication of evidence upon which to give advice.

A great deal needs to be learnt about the precise nature of the growth of trees below ground level and their effect on different kinds of shrinkable soils. Relatively speaking, very little real information of a scientific nature exists.

Usually, therefore, the professional assembles all the visible evidence presented by the crack pattern and most importantly, the time scale and sequence over which that problem has developed. He undertakes excavations to expose and identify the actual construction of foundations, the nature of the subsoil immediately beneath and the presence and type of roots in the vicinity and then forms a judgement based largely on collected experience, a capability which cannot easily be taught to others except by demonstration at the scene of incidents.

Extensive research needed

There is, therefore, a very great need for extensive research into cases of building failure caused by trees and particularly, into cases of buildings which whilst with unsound foundations by today's standards, have happily co-existed with trees of the worst kinds for years, without mishap. There must be reasons why apparently similar situations produce problems in some cases and not others. A detailed knowledge of these must lead to improvements in the quality of advice which can be given.

If we are not to consider every building built on shrinkable clay as a potentially moving object which should be made rigid by the provision of a foundation structure so massive or so complex as to totally eliminate all the extreme possibilities of movement under any excess of future weather extremes, some rational assumptions must necessarily be made and the public and the Law be encouraged to allow the professional to use his experience to judge this question of degree without fear of punitive reaction in the occasional case where some further development of distress may arise.

Preventative measures

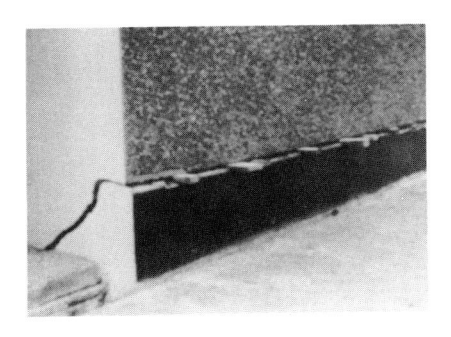

Any professional and indeed any householder should be made aware that when excessively dry or excessively wet seasons are developing, some attention to eliminating extremes in soil moisture can be prudent and useful.

Not a great deal can be done to an existing building to avoid anticipated trouble in vulnerable situations but the following can be helpful:

1. All trees within their height from the building should be pruned or pollarded to restrict their need for water. They should not be felled without careful consideration of the consequences and only after professional advice, for too rigorous cutting back can lead to expansion of soil with equally disastrous results.

2. Shrubs and substantial vegetable growth immediately adjoining buildings should be removed or cut back.

3. Ground surrounding buildings can be paved to assist in retaining such water as remains in the soil.

4. In clay soils, leaky shallow drains can be a positive advantage and in some circumstances, artificial introduction of water into soils during dry periods can be effective. This presents risks however as little is known about necessary control of such watering to prevent excessive expansion.

Leaking deep drains act as land drains and dry out soil. Improvement will result if these are repaired.

5. Any factor which goes towards the maintenance of average moisture content in subsoil under foundations throughout variable seasons, will be advantageous.

2.1 and 2.2
Trees close to house on south east Essex shrinkable clay – but . . .

structure held up without underpinning.

Adequate insurance

Particularly with domestic properties, the market climate today makes it necessary to ensure that adequate insurance cover is maintained and that it is regularly updated in these inflationary times. The sum insured must be sufficient to cover fees and Value Added Tax if applicable and should be for the replacement building cost of the structure, including drains, fences, paths, outbuildings etc. It is important to understand that the resale value is irrelevant, for very large old buildings may cost substantially more to rebuild, particularly if ancient materials and crafts are to be matched, than their contemporary open market value and conversely, a small modern prestige unit could have a market value well in excess of its rebuilding cost.

The Royal Institution of Chartered Surveyors in conjunction with the British Insurance Association have produced a booklet 'Property insurance' giving answers to many of the problem questions on insurance and also have prepared on instructions of the British Insurance Association, an analysis of the average rebuilding costs of dealing with varying classes of structure in this country (RICS Building Cost Information Service).

Many members of the insurance profession are now accepting the figures from this Service as being the basis upon which insurances should be taken out and in consequence, they may be used as evidence of under-insurance should any differences be apparent upon submission of a claim.

There is no doubt that argument is possible on any valuation and for any situation where circumstances may not be straightforward, it is strongly recommended that the sum insured be discussed with the insurance company to ensure that it is acceptable by both parties as a proper figure.

In the case of domestic policies, other than those direct from Lloyds, it is not usual for 'average' to apply. 'Average' here means

2.3
Another example of subsidence.

a percentage reduction applied to the payment of any claim in proportion to the under-insurance which is considered to have existed.

Allowing for fees & VAT

In the case of commercial properties, however, average is normal and this may be applied not at the rebuilding cost as at the date the insurance is taken out, but at the date the claim comes to be settled. In complicated cases, this can be two to three years after the assessment and an adequate recognition of potential inflation must be built into the sum insured.

The element of fees which need to be allowed for architects surveyors and engineers, will depend upon the complexity of the building being insured. As a minimum, it should be 10% and this would increase in some cases to as much as 25%.

Particularly with older and period properties, it is also important to ensure that a policy gives 'Public authority' cover which allows for re-instatement as existing, plus the cost of improving the repaired or re-instated building to comply with current regulations and requirements of local and other authorities. This may be particularly important as there is an increasing trend for local authorities to resist partial underpinning and to require the whole of any subsided building to be provided with new foundations when only a part has been disturbed. Remember, without a public authorities clause, the insurance claim might only relate to the section which shows signs of movement, leaving the building owner to pay the remainder. No two cases are exactly similar and careful professional consideration of the varying circumstances is essential in anything other than the simplest residential situation.

In all cases, sums insured must be regularly reviewed to take account of inflation.

2 A surveyor's view: Campling

The surveyor's view

Dealing to a far greater extent than many comparable professions with existing buildings, the structural surveyor tends to be rather less of an advocate of the text book solution to all building problems as it is often seen as an unreasonable burden upon whoever has to pay and a waste of resources to promote repair policies which are unjustifiably expensive in relation to the advantages obtained.

There have been many cases of massive re-instatement works specified in strict accordance with the latest recommended engineering standards which are of no practical advantage to the houseowner and place the building on an underground structure many times stronger than would have been specified by a skilled designer had the building been built for the first time in the observed conditions.

The present climate of opinion does, however, encourage the use of sledge hammers to crack nuts. An adviser cannot be criticised in law for adhering specifically to codes of practice and similar standards, whereas he can, of course, be criticised for specifying works to a lesser standard than the theoretically perfect.

In my view these present trends, whilst pursued with the best of motives, have led to extensive misery and expense to ordinary people to little practical advantage to themselves or their buildings.

More rational advice

The research and design considerations referred to by other contributors to this book are welcomed as a step towards a wider knowledge and understanding of a difficult and infinitely variable problem which can only lead to more rational advice to those unfortunate enough to own buildings which occasionally 'move' during the course of their life. There are many other causes of subsidence and building cracking which do demand major surgery but moderate seasonal differential movement is seen to be more a tactical problem judged against the background of the legal and market conditions than a technical problem which necessarily must always require immediate extensive remedial works.

3 Problems of proximity

Dr E.R.C. Reynolds

Evan R.C. Reynolds, BSc, ARCS, PhD, DIC, is Senior Research Officer and University Lecturer at the Commonwealth Forestry Institute, University of Oxford. Educated at Imperial College London, he early specialised in the relationships of water, soils, and trees, and worked for the research branch of the Forestry Commission before moving to his present post in 1958. He was recently commissioned by the Department of the Environment to review the subject of 'tree roots and built developments' to discover how much was known about the range and extent of roots and suggest what research was needed.

Most danger and nuisance from trees is above-ground (3.1), and professional or even lay survey can more often than not determine 'safe' proximities to buildings acceptable to the parties concerned. However, the contingency of modern foundation design, recent weather patterns and clay soils which shrink upon drying has given prominence to the damage by the roots of trees which are too close to buildings. In such cases it would need a major investigation to detect whether roots from neighbouring trees were approaching foundations and then to control them by methods short of destroying the trees. Furthermore, no means of root training that comes to mind would be certain of lasting success. At first sight it seemed perfectly logical then, to tackle the problem by predicting the distance at which a tree when fully grown could damage foundations, and suggest that trees on sites with at-risk soils

3.1
Most danger and nuisance . . . is above ground.

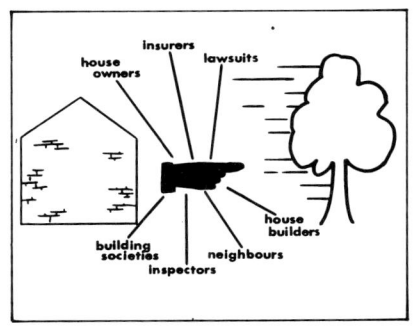

3.2
Trees versus the rest.

ought not to be allowed to be any nearer than this to a building. An inexorable series of events involving house-builders, lawsuits, insurers and building societies have served to harden such helpful advice into what some folk see as an environmental menace threatening to exclude trees from the British urban scene. Building regulations do not make such stipulations, but society has well nigh imposed such regulations on itself (3.2). Was this a right course to

Moisture 'income' and 'expenditure'

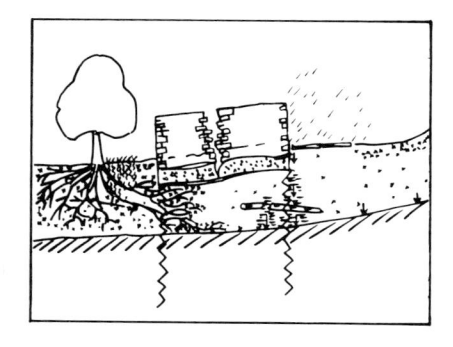

pursue, or are there alternatives to the proximity rule? To answer this we must first try to discover how roots endanger foundations.

Like many finely particulate materials, clays swell on wetting and shrink on drying. The two processes are, as a first approximation, reversible. Heave and subsidence of the surface, and damaging movements of structures founded on the soil represent the sum of different movements below them. The quantitative response of soil to changes in moisture content depends primarily upon its clay content, but is also greater the more the degree of consolidation. Unconsolidated alluvial clays form a distinct group often with considerable but only partially reversible shrinkage. The type of clay mineral is also important (crudely, the geologically older clays shrink and swell less); and the movement is affected by solutes and other colloids present or added to the soil. In the USA they are much further advanced in controlling heave and subsidence by the soil treatments which are suggested by these relationships.

Thanks to advances in modern ecology it is now easy to visualize a development site with trees on a shrinkable clay as having a balance between the various sources of income of water and the different forms of water loss. This balance, the soil moisture content, varies all the time and determines the subsidence and heave which the site experiences. Using accounting procedures (3.3) a 'running balance' can be calculated from the time course of measurements or estimates of income, such as rainfall and watering, and expenditure, such as evaporation, drainage, and abstraction by tree roots. By such means the contribution to soil movements of each of the factors in the balance can be isolated. Let us look at this in general terms.

3.3
Soil moisture accounting.

More droughts like 1976?

Our experience over the last five years has taught us that overall the most usual cause of soil movement and foundation damage has been the fluctuations of rainfall, the largest 'income' element on most sites. Is this entirely unpredictable for the coming years? Can we not use past rainfall records for which Britain is justly famed, to peer into the future? My colleague, Dr Denis Alder, has suggested on the basis of past rainfall, that we may expect a drought of the intensity of 1976 sometime in the next fifty years, but that a season very much dryer is unlikely.

Rainfall will only wet the shrinkable soil if its infiltration is not prevented by paving. We know rather little about the effects of the common urban soil coverings on the soil environment from the viewpoint of the moisture content or tree health. Sometimes paving will shed water to the shrinkable clay soil beneath foundations and diminish settlement. Some say that paving causes extension of tree roots with the possibility of damage being caused by greater distances from the tree trunk. I have yet to see convincing data supporting this idea.

Shrink and heave

Still on the income side of the water balance of the soil, moisture may be received *via* the water table. This is related to the topographical environs of the site. I have hypothesized that in a situation where there is a long and not too steep clay slope above, soil moisture will be maintained even in a drought and settlement damage would be unlikely. Likewise old field drains on a development site convey extra water to the shrinkable soil.

Leaking mains, storm and foul-water sewers will augment soil moisture and preclude shrinking locally. Repairing these services and thus allowing the clay to dry and shrink has been known to be the prelude to building damage. Tree roots often proliferate if in their 'random walk' they reach one of these sources of water and nutrients. It could be that a tree thus supplied adequately with water would have a less extensive root system and that it would never dry the soil intensively beneath the foundations of an adjacent building.

Turning to the other side of the balance sheet, water may be lost from the site by drainage to the water table and sub-surface flow in the saturated zone. Soil above the water table tends towards an equilibrium moisture content which, in our conditions, would not be associated with significant shrinkage from the saturated state. Evaporation on the other hand, can dry the clay soil well below the shrinkage limit. However, as the top soil dries, it is 'self-mulching', so that in Britain shrinkage due to evaporation from bare soil would rarely produce damaging shrinkage where foundations were deeper than, say 50cm. But shrinkable clay soils raise a complication — the system of cracks produced by their lateral shrinkage which forms barriers to water movement as well as routes for infiltrating water and evaporation.

Roots dry out soil

Root activity amounts, in effect, to an extension of the evaporating surface to various depths in the soil. Plants are able to dry clay soils within the root range to around the dryness of the shrinkage limit. But how extensive is the root range? The vertical depth determines the amount of subsidence the plants produce, and the lateral extent the distance from the shoot base to which they will cause soil shrinkage. In this way drying may penetrate under the edge of pavements or buildings. While water is available in the soil, the rate of drying is dependent on, and can be calculated from, the drying power of the atmosphere. The amount of water available depends on the soil type and the rooted volume. The range of the roots of trees and other plants is thus seen to be a vital parameter in comprehending their role in soil subsidence, and is implicitly used as the basis for the rules of thumb for safe proximities of trees to buildings on shrinkable clay.

But I contend that to observe the roots by excavation is far from ideal for our purposes. We wish to know the limits of the vertical and horizontal extent; Therefore holes within these limits are of little interest. Rooting may be sparse towards the margins of the root range. What density of roots would be effective in drying the soil, bearing in mind that the active roots may be no more than

2mm in diameter? Then again, can we be sure that the roots we observe are alive and actively absorbing water?

More research needed

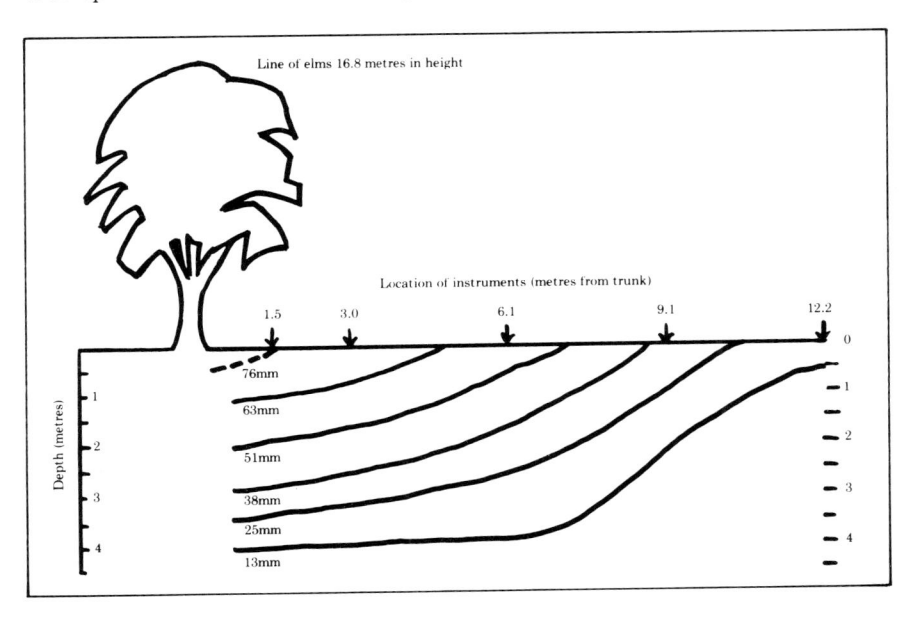

What I advise as appropriate for our purpose is direct observation of the depth, spread and intensity of soil drying around a plant, preferably combined with subsidence measurements. In Chapter 4, Dr Biddle presents some preliminary observations which I feel confirm my view that these are the data upon which valid advice on tree proximity can be based. Such investigations cannot be hurried, because observations probably have to span a reasonably dry summer.

But has this work never been done before? When I look at the published literature, I find that under British climatic conditions, in the shrinkable soils which occur in these islands and with the tree species which we commonly use in urban planting, there are

3.4
Vertical subsidence of leda clay, Ottawa, Canada (Burn & Penner 1975) caused by elm trees in 1955
(tree drawn one-third scale).

only a couple of strictly relevant investigations. From these and other less apt sets of data, I can only make the rather negative observation that I have no reason to believe that when more research is conducted this will necessitate altering the current guidelines to decrease or increase the distances from buildings for safe planting. But at least research could evince confidence instead of scepticism about the advice. I believe that it cannot but do further harm to attitudes towards the urban tree to redefine the recommendations on proximity, or even to reiterate those we already have, *without* any improvement in our knowledge through research. Whether or not an adequate amount of research will ever be done depends whether, in a competitive financial climate, government makes funds available for this rather than other research (3.4).

Unpredictable

The guidelines presuppose that the rooting of trees is reasonably regular, not highly eccentric, and also that relative to some easily estimated parameter, such as tree height, root spread is sufficiently predictable to incorporate into the advice without some unacceptably large safety margin. I am not convinced that these points can be met, and so I continue by looking for an alternative solution to the problem rather than having to admit some rule of proximity.

Only shrinkable clays

The extant recommendations, and any others in the future that rely only on our present knowledge base, carry a number of important caveats which have been largely disregarded and thus the guidelines are thought to be more stringent than they actually are. Some of the alleged effects of the advice detrimental to the urban environment have arisen from superficial acquaintance with the documents. I refer to such provisos as that the advice *relates only to soils which can be classed as shrinkable clays and no others*. References to the mature height of the tree as a useful correlate for deciding on the adjacency of tree and building take no account of arboricultural techniques for preventing the tree growing too large, of the restricted growth on certain sites or of certain smaller varieties of the tree species.

Effort in making these limitations to the applicability of the guidelines widely known amongst property owners, builders, building societies, planners and such like, would go some way to redressing the mistaken attitudes that have arisen. Additionally propaganda stressing the aesthetic value of the urban tree and of the ease with which much of the damage ascribable to root activity can be repaired would further alleviate people's doubts.

Foundations, not trees

Allusion has already been made to management of the tree crown, and Dr Biddle ascribes some damage by street trees to the false economy of neglecting regular pruning. By reducing the size of the tree crown, the water needs of the tree would probably be smaller and consequently the drying of the soil less. Looking at the soil/plant/weather/building as a single system, it seems strange that we should ever have thought of approaching the protection of the building through regulating the proximity of trees. With biological variability as it is, our lack of knowledge of the factors which control the development of root systems, the difficulty of locating active roots, our inexperience in manipulating root spread, and the likelihood of 'volunteer' trees springing up close to a building, any alternative approach would seem to be preferable. On the other hand, a building's foundations are far more amenable to control and can be accommodated to site contingencies. The most easily varied parameter is the foundation depth along with introducing the economies of piles. Local treatment of the subsoil to reduce subsidence has not even been considered yet in connection with the problem in Britain. The flexibility of the foundation and superstructure has never been adjusted to cope with the contingency of active roots in the subsoil. Research into these engineering alternatives is likely to be more rewarding than 'biological' investigations, especially if efforts are made to build as cheaply as with conventional methods.

Cheaper, more sensible solutions

Turning to the problem of trees near existing buildings, private enterprise has developed methods of stabilizing foundations which have suffered damaging settlement. There has been little encouragement to seek cheaper yet effective methods to do this, but I think we are likely to see these developments as competition in the industry grows.

What can we say about preventing damage to existing buildings as trees grow up alongside them? This is a situation where, if the foundations are shallow and the soil is definitely shrinkable, perhaps tree crowns could be reduced according to the distance from the building if this is proved to prevent excessive drying by tree roots.

There is no need to pretend that trees are not frequently wholly or partly to blame for settlement damage to buildings on shrinkable clay, but there is no reason why we should be content to allow the potential of trees to damage buildings to banish trees from the urban landscape. Engineering ways of preventing or repairing damage are feasible, but means should be devised to do so economically. Arboricultural methods may also become available. However, without spending money on relevant building and arboricultural research and on observing the drying and shrinking patterns around trees, it is difficult to see how the trend towards treeless towns can be reversed.

4 Practical tests and conclusions

Dr Giles Biddle

P. Giles Biddle, MA, DPhil, read forestry at Oxford, then studied for a doctorial thesis on virus diseases of forest trees before spending a post-doctorial year at the University of California, Berkeley. After two further years of research at Oxford, he left to launch his own firm, Tree Conservation Ltd, as an arboricultural consultant. After initially concentrating on Dutch elm disease, the consultancy has lately specialised in problems of tree root damage to buildings on shrinkable clays, and Dr Biddle was consultant to the steering committee for the Department of the Environment's research project 'tree roots and built developments'. He is vice-chairman of the Arboricultural Association, and serves on the standing committee on Arboricultural Education and on the Forestry Training Council.

If we are to minimize the risk of trees causing structural damage to properties, it is essential that we should understand the mechanisms involved in such damage. Knowledge about these mechanisms can come from theoretical considerations, from case study observations of the behaviour of buildings in the proximity to trees, and from research (4.1, 4.2).

4.1
Mature trees can greatly enhance suburban streets . . .

4.2
. . . lack of them produces a prairie-like appearance.

Dr Reynolds has mentioned some of the theoretical considerations, emphasising the importance of water in the system. It is the balance between water input and water loss that is critical. In the absence of trees, water input from rainfall from lateral and vertical accession and from leaking drains is likely to be in approximate balance with the water losses from evaporation, surface run off and drainage. There may be some minor seasonal fluctuations, but these will only affect the surface layers of soil. However, a tree will lose water as transpiration from the leaf surface, and this water is obtained by the roots absorbing it from the soil. This absorption can occur from the deeper soil levels, including those beneath the foundations. If the soil is a clay, this can produce soil shrinkage, with the amount of this dependent on the clay chemistry, texture, particle size and geological history. As the clay soils differ in these properties, there will be differences in the amount of soil shrinkage, and also differences in the soil permeability can influence the water movements which correct any deficit produced by root activity.

Estimating 'water deficit'

I would now like to compare these theoretical considerations with the results from various site investigations, and the preliminary results of some research projects. I should make it clear that by site investigation I am referring to investigations following structural damage to buildings, as opposed to the investigations of site conditions which should be made prior to development.

The emphasis of site investigations should be on the water balance and the effects of this on the soil and the building. As we are normally concerned with soil shrinkage and damage occurring during the extremes of dry weather, the ideal is to measure the soil moisture content during these conditions. This can be easily achieved by drilling boreholes, and then measuring the soil moisture content by simple laboratory methods. In this way, provided there is a reasonably homogeneous soil, it is possible to compare the moisture content profile in the vicinity of the tree with conditions away from the influence of the tree, and from this determine the soil moisture deficit produced by the tree. Such measurements of moisture deficits can indicate both the lateral and vertical extent of the influence of the tree roots.

Unfortunately, it is rarely possible to investigate conditions on the precise date when deficits are at their maximum and it is then necessary to estimate it on the basis of experience. On the heavy clay soils with low permeability the process of rehydration can be very slow. Thus, in the spring of 1977 it was still possible to measure water deficits which developed during 1976 below a depth of about 1.5 metres on the London clay, whereas on the more permeable sandy clays these were rapidly corrected. Once the soil has rehydrated, it is still possible to examine the soil very carefully for the fine moisture-absorbing roots, and on the basis of experience estimate the amount of water deficit that these would have produced. In this context it should be emphasised that the large roots usually taken for identification purposes would be used solely for water conduction rather than absorption, and they may not necessarily be

4.3
A sample of fine oak roots.

functional. The presence of these large roots is not therefore indicative of moisture absorption, and it is far more relevant to determine the depth and rooting density of the living fine roots (4.3).

Some clays more 'shrinkable' than others

It has been emphasised that clay soils will differ in their shrinkability, depending on their chemical and physical properties and their geological origin. In order to establish the amount of soil shrinkage produced by a tree, it is therefore necessary to correlate the soil water deficit with shrinkage. Surprisingly there is no simple direct laboratory test of the natural shrinkage properties of a soil. The oedometer uses undisturbed core soil samples and can measure vertical soil expansion or contraction but it cannot make any allowance for horizontal movements. Other methods make no attempt to measure the natural soil conditions, but attempt to estimate shrinkage properties from other soil characteristics.

It can be shown that there is a very close linear correlation between plasticity index and percentage linear shrinkage, suggesting that, until more acceptable methods are developed, these provide the best method of placing a soil in a category of shrinkability. Using plasticity index (PI) as a basis of classification, I would suggest that a PI less than 25 indicates low shrinkability, between 25 and 50 moderate shrinkability, and PI greater than 50 indicates a highly shrinkable soil. I would suggest that even such a simple classification system as this would emphasise the enormous difference between soils such as the boulder clay (PI variable but usually 15-20) compared with the highly shrinkable London clay (PI usually 50-70). All these clays tend at present to be described as 'shrinkable', and the same rule relating tree size to proximity to buildings is applied. Each soil deserves to be judged on its own merits.

Inconsistent with allegations

Although it may be impossible to define the precise shrinkage, once the water deficit is known it is possible to estimate the amount of shrinkage, and by measuring the water deficit beneath the foundations to estimate the maximum amount of subsidence which might have been produced by the tree. Even with the highly shrinkable London clay and the worst water deficits produced by a large poplar tree, it would be unusual for this shrinkage to be more than 100mm (4 inches). With other tree species, and obviously dependent on the distance from the tree, shrinkage is unlikely to be more than 30mm.

These amounts of soil shrinkage can be compared with the actual subsidence by measuring the level of the building. If it is assumed that a building is usually constructed with level brickcourses (and observation on modern undamaged buildings or old buildings on stable subsoils confirms that they are usually within 10mm of level), the divergence from level can indicate the direction and extent of differential foundation movements. In my opinion accurate measurement of the level of a basal brickcourse is a fundamental stage in any site investigation. In many cases I have found that it demonstrates that the patterns of building movement are totally inconsistent with allegations that trees have caused subsidence. Sometimes, particularly on the glacial and alluvial soils, it can be shown that the maximum subsidence has occurred in parts of the building not adjacent to the trees. In other cases the levels demonstrate that parts of a building are heaving either as a result of tree removal or from the dieback of a root system which often occurs following site development. If observations of the level of a building agree with the measurements of soil shrinkage, it provides strong evidence of the probable involvement of the tree. Such evidence is of far greater value than attempting to deduce the building movements from examination of the pattern of cracking.

Crack monitoring

One common result from such an examination is to find that the direction of movement indicates the involvement of a tree, but the amount of movement is far greater than the shrinkage. This usually occurs where foundations are particularly shallow or the load bearing properties of the soil are on the limit of safety. Each summer the tree may cause soil shrinkage and subsidence, but when

4.4
Accurate measurement of movement in brickwork can often show clearly that trees are, or are not, responsible.

that soil rehydrates the swelling pressures result in either consolidation or *sheer failure* of the soil. In this way the subsidence becomes progressively worse each year until finally damage occurs. Legally in these situations the tree would probably be held 100% liable, despite the fact that the damage would not have developed if the foundations had been properly designed for these conditions.

Some indication of this progressive failure can be gained by monitoring crack movements using an accurate measure such as a Demec strain gauge or vernier calipers. Crack movements produced solely by soil shrinkage and swelling will show a regular seasonal fluctuation whereas cracks caused by foundation settlement, clay creep or other causes will show a progressive increase in crack width or different pattern of movement.

I would also suggest that accurate crack monitoring (4.4) could often prevent the necessity for extensive repairs. If it is agreed that a tree has caused damage, removal of the tree or curtailment of its water demand should eliminate any further seasonal movements although some heave might occur. If measurements can demonstrate that significant movements have ceased, it indicates that remedial work could reasonably be limited to cosmetic repairs without the necessity for expensive underpinning or similar works.

I would emphasise that such measurements must be accurate and that the use of glass or concrete telltales, usually inadequately fixed, is a waste of time and effort and merely indicates the lack of professionalism of its user.

Tree species – mistaken generalisations

I have described some of the techniques which I use and these usually provide a clear indication of the degree of involvement of a tree as a cause of damage. Based on these techniques, out of two hundred cases of damage which I have investigated during the past three years, I consider that trees were fully liable in 50% of cases, partially liable with some other major contributory factor in 32% of cases, and contributing to less than 10% of the damage in 18% of cases. Obviously these percentages would vary in different parts of the country, with very much higher values on the London clay, but lower values on some of the other soils, notably glacial boulder clay.

A persistent theme in descriptive texts on structural damage caused by trees is that certain 'fast-growing forest trees' are more likely to cause damage. Poplar, willow and elm are often cited as examples (eg in Department of Environment PSA, Technical Instruction Serial 128, December 1976 'Foundations on shrinkable and swelling clays'). The results of measurements of soil moisture deficits during site investigations confirm that poplar produces far greater and more extensive water deficits than other species, but personally I have had no occasion to investigate willow and have my doubts whether it is as demanding in its water requirements. What is apparent is that fast-growing species are not necessarily the most damaging. For instance, I would suggest that comparatively rapid growing species such as horse chestnut and silver birch have a low water demand, whereas the slow growing whitebeam, whose small size makes it ideal for street planting, can produce damage almost comparable to a poplar. On the basis of site investigations and observations, I would suggest that species can be listed (in descending order of likelihood of causing damage) as follows: poplar, Lombardy poplar, *Cupressus macrocarpa,* whitebeam, hawthorn, oak, elm, ash, lime, plane, sycamore, birch and beech.

Neutron probes

During the past year I have started a project for the Milton Keynes Development Corporation to study these effects. So far this has been restricted to sorting out the best methods, in particular comparing rod gauges for direct measurement of soil shrinkage, and the neutron probe for measurement of changes in the soil moisture content. The neutron probe is already providing some interesting data and would appear to be the ideal tool for this work.

The probe requires holes drilled into the soil to the required depth

4.5
Plastic-lined boreholes into which an oedometer can be lowered when required.

4.6
The author taking readings by means of a borehole.

(about 3m) and at varying distances from the tree. These holes are lined with aluminium tubes (4.5), down which the probe can be lowered. The probe contains a small sealed radioactive source emitting fast neutrons. If these neutrons collide with a hydrogen atom, they are slowed down and reflected, and the probe contains a counter for these slow returning neutrons. As virtually the sole source of hydrogen atoms in the soil is in the form of water, the count of returning neutrons is proportional to the soil moisture content. This neutron probe is therefore particularly valuable for measuring changes in soil moisture, particularly as repeated readings can be made in a single access hole (4.6), whereas soil sampling requires a fresh hole each time which interferes with the normal drainage patterns.

The pilot study during this past year has only investigated one tree each of lime and horse chestnut on Oxford and on boulder clays and with only 3 tubes per tree. With these species on these soils, during

1978 the water deficits barely extended below a depth of 1m even at a distance of 0.4 x tree height, and the horse chestnut showed no effect at 0.8 x tree height on either soil type. The results also show that even the brief period of heavy rain in late July was sufficient to correct most of the water deficit.

I believe that if this technique can be extended to cover a wide variety of species, and to study the influence of different soil types on the pattern of water deficits and shrinkage, in the future it should provide more precise information on acceptable safe distances between trees and buildings.

Regular pruning needed

Species selection might provide a valuable tool in the future, but where trees already exist close to buildings and are likely to cause damage, an alternative approach is required. It has been noted that the transpirational water losses are related to leaf area, and it is possible to control this leaf area by pruning. The effects of this are exemplified by many of the plane and lime trees on the London streets. Prior to the 1970's, there was a policy of regular annual or bi-annual pollarding which removed virtually all of the shoots and leaf area. Growth rate and water demand was minimal, but the trees looked diabolical and therefore, at the insistence of many local amenity societies and with welcome economies in the local authority pruning budget, the trees were allowed to develop a larger and more attractive crown area. Water demand and growth rate shot up, and I suggest that many of these trees were likely to cause damage during any reasonably dry summer, without requiring the extremes of 1976.

We are now investigating the effect of different pruning regimes to try to strike a balance between acceptable appearance and reasonable water demand which will not cause damage (4.7, 4.8). We know that we can control growth rate in this way, and thus by implication the water demand, but it will also be necessary to determine the pattern of water demand of these different pruning regimes. The neutron probe should prove a valuable tool in this research.

4.7
General view of plane trees in the Fortis Green district of Haringey, showing appearance of heavy pruning.

4.8
General view (in the same area as 4.7) showing appearance of light pruning.

5 Keeping and planting trees on development sites

Ivor Cunningham

Ivor Cunningham, AADip, RIBA, DipLA(Dunelm), AILA, is an architect and landscape architect educated in Britain and Holland. He worked in the offices of Brenda Colvin, Sylvia Crowe, and Eric Anjou in Stockholm, before joining Eric Lyons' architectural practice in 1955. He became a partner in 1960, and has been involved in all the practice's design work, but with special responsibility for landscape, including notably its Span housing estates.

'*The stately homes of England,
How beautiful they stand
Amidst their tall ancestral trees
O'er all the pleasant land.*'

Felicia Dorothea Hemans' early nineteenth century sentiment expressed no sign of conflict between the house and its trees, only the complementary values they have for each other. Our modern lives seem to be dominated by conflicts of one kind or another, and on the particular subject of trees it is the pressure on land and the rise of consumer power that is placing the professional adviser and his love of trees in some difficulty. The shadow of claims for professional negligence as interpreted by Lord Denning and others in the judiciary will inevitably make us much more circumspect when giving advice or instruction about tree conservation where new building is contemplated.

Worse than Dutch elm disease

Nan Fairbrother in her book *New lives, new landscapes* put forward the view that trees will diminish in numbers in the countryside due to agricultural economics, and it is at the extremes of forest planting on the poorer soils on one hand and in the built up areas on the other that trees will be found in abundance. It is the latter which affects most people most of the time and wherein now lies the greatest danger to our total landscape scenery. If the attitudes now being canvassed and legalised by the 'Building Safety Conglomerate' are logically and ruthlessly pursued then our towns will become disaster areas that will suffer more than the low land countryside did after the ravages of the elm beetle.

Our towns consist mainly of housing of one kind or another and their land is subject to a greater intensity of use than almost any other building category. This factor magnifies some of the disadvantages of trees including the possible effect of their root system on building foundations and underground services.

Trees fall over or drop their branches, they are struck by lightning, leaves block gutters and gullies and much labour is required in Autumn clearing up the leaves. There are dangers to people and vehicles bumping into trees, children falling out of them and kittens getting stuck up them. Never mind the general mess that seems to emanate from trees and their wild life.

Some of the troubles are occasional or trivial, others however can be of a continuous nature and must be planned for at the beginning of a new project where trees exist on the site.

Trees are our visual links

Most people, at least civilised people, are quite convinced that the advantages of conserving trees far outweigh the disadvantages (5.1).

5.1
Templemere, Weybridge
Preservation of line of large cedars and other trees. Building groups designed to diffuse space.

Trees are the primary visual links between land, buildings and the sky, the most prominent of all plant life, and without their presence our townscapes would be naked. A sense of continuity is given by old trees and they remain well known landmarks when unneeded buildings, hedgerows and paths make way for new developments. The retention of existing trees will obviously help to create an immediate settled landscape to a new housing estate and they are also much more likely to survive the impact of young people's activities. Most trees will take a number of years to reach maturity so that new planting will look sparse and lilliputian for a number of years. Nevertheless, new planting must be carried out to ensure the continuity of tree life into the future. The irregular shape of trees, their colour and texture, is a necessary complement to the inorganic nature of building.

All plants have some characteristics akin to man in their growth and change, their response to the seasons (except that they mostly lose their vestments when we add to ours in winter), and have occasional bouts of unpredictable behaviour. Trees have the added desire for dominance which is perhaps what St Mark meant when he wrote 'I see men as trees, walking' (Chap VIII, v. 24).

Trees can sell houses

In visual terms, existing trees will help to screen or restrict undesirable views, enlarge the landscape scale by diffusing site boundaries, and relate to other trees on adjoining land.

In practical terms the retention of trees can give privacy, act as windbreaks, reduce outside noise (at least in psychological terms), stabilise soil on sloping ground and they can modify ground temperatures, reducing frost or excessive heat.

Before any design work is done on a project it is important that the client as well as the architect appreciates the value of retaining trees for environmental and sales reasons. Such values are difficult to

Keeping and planting trees on development sites: Cunningham

5.2
Corner Green, Blackheath
Photograph taken before the scheme was completed and shows a tree left very near an entrance porch. The tree is still there (at least it was last year) and has grown much larger. Obviously liked by the house owner.

5.3
Over Minnis, New Ash Green
Walnut trees in the foreground. Soil is clay on chalk.

quantify (like all aesthetics) but they should be allowed for at the beginning and possible extra costs taken into account.

The local planning authority will most likely make a list of trees to be preserved, particularly where they have been planted in prominent positions, and they are likely to be the oldest and largest of the specimens. These are not always the most desirable ones to keep and the Planning Officer may have to be persuaded to list other and younger trees if a healthy future is to be achieved. To my knowledge the preservation of trees cannot be considered a good reason in itself for withholding planning permission but it would be surprising if many or most trees could not be retained by careful planning. Neighbours can also be sensitive to the removal of existing trees particularly when they have relied on yours for privacy and pleasure rather than wasting their own land for such bulky objects (5.2).

Happily cheek by jowl

The preparation of an accurate site survey is vital to good planning. Not only are the contours and natural features to be plotted but the position, spread and types of trees must be noted. This should be followed up by a site visit to discover any anomalies and to check the health of the trees and the soil structure. In the site planning of buildings a tree or group of trees can take on a fresh and important role in the newly created environment. Some trees need space to display their true natures while others can settle snugly in smaller areas cheek by jowl with the buildings. Often some ingenuity is demanded in planting the dwellings, shaping the roads and paths and threading the underground services in and out of the clumps of trees to get a satisfactory result (5.3). The present climate for low rise buildings and for houses instead of flats has meant less 'public' space for trees. More land is given over to private gardens and a tree that gets enclosed in such an area may not survive very long if the occupier decides that it is too big for his patch.

Often a decision has to be made in deciding what tree or trees have to be sacrificed for the greater gain. This may take on the nature of a game of chess and some specialist advice could be valuable in making the right moves. It is possible to move smaller trees to new situations if carried out during the winter and a healthy root ball is maintained. Care must always be taken to protect trees from the excesses of the building contractor, whether they get in the way of his machinery, his stock piling or his bonfires. Very often a healthy cost penalty can temper his actions.

Deeper foundations demanded

The general problem of soils will be dealt with more than adequately in the other chapters and I will restrict my contribution to some brief comments on the practical aspects of trees and building foundations. As far as the stability of buildings are concerned they can be placed as close to trees as may be wished on almost any soil. It is a question of foundation design and cost. On many soils and sub-soils such as gravel, sand, light loams and chalks there is generally little in the way of a foundation problem unless thirsty trees like

5.4
Westfield, The Marld, Ashtead
Site of heavy clay soil. Photograph taken on completion. Trees still there.

Protecting trees against buildings

poplars, thorns, ash, or the late-lamented elms are nearby. The villains in the woodpile are the shrinkable clays and some chalk sub-soils which change volume according to the season and rainfall. Many, if not most, serious construction faults in private housing have been due to inadequate foundations and it is not surprising that district surveyors, building inspectors and the National House-Building Council have become extremely cautious of late and are demanding deeper foundations to a state of overkill where not even the smallest possible risk can be taken. One side effect to our advantage is that there is not the same problem of the proximity of the buildings to the new tree planting (5.4). A recent development of ours for replacing 3- and 4-storey houses by 2-storey and attic room houses has some 50 feet deep piles thrust through the clay. The original houses had survived for 150 years with almost no foundations to speak of.

On shrinkable clays piling or mass concrete foundations sunk below the tree root layer would give the best protection against soil movement. Alternatively a tree can be isolated by some local trench sheeting if considered too near to a building. The avoidance of strong cement mortars and the use of 1:1:6 cement/lime/cement mix for external brickwork and even 1:2:9 mix for internal brick or block work would allow some gentle settlement without producing unsightly fissures in the brickwork. As an alternative, lightweight or framed structures with cladding that can 'rack' would certainly reduce the effect of differential ground movement.

One particular precaution worth taking on doubtful soils is to consult a sympathetic structural engineer well versed in soil conditions.

Drains can be affected by movement of shrinkable clays particularly where trees are present and they can be given extra protection by increasing their depth in the ground, by surrounding them in mass concrete or by using flexible pipes and jointing systems.

5.5
Brackley, Weybridge
Lime avenue retained.

Besides the effect of trees on buildings the reverse has to be considered. Care must be taken not to remove too much of the root system. Generally speaking it is considered possible for a quarter of the roots to be removed and still maintain the tree in good health. In all cases the soil around trees should be maintained at the original levels, but where severe changes have to be made, retaining walls about 10 feet away from the tree can be built provided enough of the root system is kept.

Trees are like people who, when young, can adapt to new situations, but in old age must stick to the good old ways. A balanced society has a place for the old as well as the young and I think that such a view of society should be mirrored in our housing landscapes by retaining the existing trees as well as planting new specimens (5.5).

6 Planting trees on bare housing sites

Neil Higson

R. Neil Higson, AILA, studied landscape architecture under Frank Clark at Reading University, then worked for Kent County Council, the LCC, Essex County Council, moving to Basildon New Town in 1964. In the following year he became Principal Landscape Architect to Basildon New Town. After starting a landscape design division in Manchester's City Architect's Department, he started a private landscape practice, Neil & Pirkko Higson & Associates, in Stoney Stratford in 1975, which designed housing landscapes for Milton Keynes and (for Salveson) at Delamere Park, Cheshire. In 1977 he resigned from the practice to become Chief Landscape Architect to Milton Keynes Development Corporation.

It is possible, if somewhat costly, to achieve pockets of instant landscape on bare sites. Semi-mature trees, turf, large container grown shrubs and specially prepared climbers can be used to present the show house area very favourably to prospective purchasers, future tenants and the architectural press.

The problem of creating a rich landscape overall is more complex. On every green field site there is a resource at least as valuable as the hundred year old Cedar tree, or the mature Oak – that is, the topsoil and natural drainage pattern.

Topsoil is consistently wasted by mishandling. Construction contractors drive heavy machines over it, destroying its structure. Sometimes it is never stripped. It may be stripped in bad weather conditions, stored badly and mixed with subsoil, or simply lost. Good topsoil can mean a difference of 9in. a year in tree growth, and its careful conservation must be a prime rule, particularly on bare sites. Parts of the site can be left undisturbed and fenced off. Soil stripping should be restricted to dry conditions and topsoil stacks should be fenced in and kept clean.

Effective pioneers

The creation of landscape which is quickly effective also depends on the selection of plants that grow reliably and vigorously in the locally prevailing conditions, rather than plants with delightful qualities which stand still or struggle for years to realise the designer's effects. Refined horticultural collections or purist ecological solutions can delay the achievement of a respected landscape and, on bare sites, the new landscape will require all the care and respect it can get from residents. The best defence against vandalism is abundant healthy growth. In Colin Ward's programme in the recent BBC television series 'Where we live now', Runcorn was referred to as the new town without vandalism. Our early worry there was that planting would be destroyed, but it has become well established and popular with the inhabitants (6.1).

6.1
Runcorn – solution to vandalism.
A place for freedom and enjoyment.

6.2
The Brow, Runcorn
Transcending the site boundary to achieve richness, maturity and a sense of place.

6.3
The Brow, Runcorn
Tenants add the decorative dimension to a rich landscape setting produced by the development corporation.

If a new housing landscape is to succeed it must be noticeably effective in the first year. It must not obviously deteriorate and it must reach a degree of maturity in the first three years after planting. It is possible to use successions of plants to achieve this result, for instance, rapid growing willows, poplars and elders can be used as part of the structure planting of a housing area in intimate mixtures with slower growing species, and can be selectively removed to enable the slower growing species to take over eventually. Two stages of planting design occur in this approach, and some of the species most successful at creating an atmosphere of early maturity can be a problem later if used indiscriminately. Landscape is always a dynamic design problem which cannot be divorced from maintenance/management. This implies a degree of constant imaginative attention which is sometimes difficult to achieve in both public and private housing. If it is to function adequately, however, the landscape design profession must be prepared to stay with schemes during their evolution and develop relationships with maintenance groups which ensure pursuit of a common objective.

Wall-to-wall landscape

It is often possible on bare sites to conserve local character by relating to features beyond the site, the history and colours of the area and its trees, hedges and copses. If the site boundary can be transcended in this way, external features and characteristics can help add maturity and richness to new development, above all achieving the sense of place so lacking in many standard box-housing schemes (6.2).

The Brow housing area in Runcorn has been often described, and various aspects of it have been emulated from its narrow roads to its monopitch roofs. It was once a bare site except for a few hedges, a pond and a group of trees in one corner. It is now a mature looking estate set in a very rich landscape to which the individual gardening efforts of tenants add the decorative dimension. Trees are an essential part of its landscape quality, but there were many more facets to the original concept (6.3).

The beauty of most woodland derives not only from its dominant tree canopy, but from its shrub and herb layers also. The beauty of an English country lane is a combination of the movement route, verges with grass and flowers, hedges and trees. The Brow landscape set out to use this range of qualities as a setting for simple rental housing.

Planting as a buffer

The roads and paths base their form on the character of lanes in and approaching an adjoining village (6.4). Thanks to the support of a unique engineer, the principle of slow movement of vehicles on narrow curving roads was accepted and allowed a pedestrian/vehicle movement pattern totally compatible with the land form and new landscape of the place. Earth from house slabs and roads was formed into banks around gardens, and was planted with strong hedges. Car parking was arranged in small cells structured with naturalistic plant masses. All incompatible uses were separated with planting masses, and trees were used to unify the whole setting (6.5). Individual residents can carry on their own activities within this landscape matrix without dominating the neighbourhood. Even the inevitable crop of decaying new town cars is absorbed without detriment to the general atmosphere.

6.4
Roads base their form on the character of lanes approaching the adjoining village of Halton.

6.5
Incompatible uses separated by plant masses, trees unifying the setting.

During the early design stages of the Brow one was so pre-occupied with the need to quickly establish an abundant landscape that the possibility of trees growing well enough to damage houses was ignored. There was a general feeling that problems arising from plants growing well would be very pleasant to have. Many rapid growing species were used, and some pruning has occurred to avoid shading windows. The scheme is not built on shrinkable clay, and there has been no root damage as yet. With sympathetic maintenance, it appears to be evolving well as a garden estate; but panic by the managing authority fired by an over cautious and generalised British Standard could destroy what 'Merseyside vandals' have learned to live with and enjoy.

Framework plantations

The Brow is a housing area of 280+ houses and, although there is a substantial central open space and a high tree content to the scheme, it does somewhat lack major framework plantations. Since in some areas it is prudent to restrain planting of many quick growing and forest trees in close proximity to houses, framework plantation copses and tree belts became an even more important part of the setting of public and private housing.

Whenever such measures are proposed, the reaction of local authorities tends to be to keep them to an absolute minimum since they become public open space and their maintenance has to be carried out by already overloaded public works departments. The standard of maintenance that is considered for costing purposes by the local authority is often something approaching that of a municipal park. Natural evolving woodland can be a most effective means of upgrading a neighbourhood, and its management can amount to little more than annual rubbish clearance leaving resources available to apply a more manicured approach to key parts of the scheme (6.6).

6.6
Heavily planted housing area landscape — management amounts to little more than litter clearance.

Are we afraid of trees' vitality?

Alternatives to local authority maintenance, for instance, residents' associations and open space trusts, can also ensure the achievement of a scale of housing area landscape which exceeds that of the private garden. Local authority ecologists, landscape architects and maintainers could well offer advice and help to these associations, thereby substantially increasing the range of open space character achieved in their area.

Smaller belts of structural planting can be absorbed into individual ownership. Very young trees are, however, likely to be swept away by the avid property owner. Larger trees obtain more respect, and a recently suggested approach to protect young plantations is to sell them to the house purchaser but for the local authority to lease them back for a period of 5 years. Both use patterns and planting should have become well established by the end of this period.

So vehement has the cry against trees and landscapes become since the drought years that one suspects that a substantial section of society is intimidated by the uncontrolled vitality of landscape and plants, and would be far more reassured in an environment totally composed of dead materials. Some builders have been most anxious to avoid the additional worries of having trees on their estates, insurance agents have witheld cover where trees are near houses, and the National House-Building Council have sympathetically emphasised their standards on trees in relation to buildings.

A safe approach to planting

Certainly, there is cause for anxiety, but there is such a variation in behaviour of different tree species that it is essential to understand which trees are the 'villains'. It is also important not to over-react on soils which are not vulnerable to shrinkage. More landscape design care will be necessary in certain parts of the country, but I think it is possible to produce housing environment which will appear as rich as parts of Letchworth and Welwyn Garden City without worrying the house owner or over-reaching the insurance companies.

To achieve this, three planting categories can be used:
— Firstly, framework planting well away from buildings, as suggested above;
— Secondly, zones of planting in which vertical membranes are used to confine root growth. Service/drain trenches can sometimes be conveniently used as locations for such protection;
— Finally, the area close to the building in which 'safe' species of trees and shrubs must be used and soil conditions can be modified if necessary to support these. Birch is probably the safest tree, and it is not happy on heavy clay.

Further implications of this approach are that good landscape schemes will take more design time and will cost more. It will also necessitate landscape designers being involved at a fundamental level in housing area layout design (no bad thing for other reasons also). The 'standard box' tendency in both rent and sale housing emphasises the need for the rich green setting if environmental quality and sense of place are to be achieved.

One per cent more

At Delamere Park, the rich landscape of Phase 1 is helping to sell the rest of the scheme, and a fair number of the same developer's houses in other areas as well.

The green setting may not be the first thing the new house purchaser puts on his shopping list, but it is a quality from which sooner or later he or his family will derive peace, pleasure and delight. To protect his investment and still have rich landscape around his home may cost a little more. Since housing area planting cost seldom amounts to more than two per cent of the house cost at present, and is more often less than one per cent, there will be little hardship to anyone in doubling present housing area landscape allowances.

7 Trees in the wider landscape

Paul Walshe

Paul Nicholas Walshe, RIBA, AILA, ARIAS, was educated at Douai, the Benedictine monastery, farm and public school in Berkshire, then studied architecture at Oxford, and practised it in Paris (Binoux et Foliasson) and London (Casson Conder & Partners). After studying environmental conservation at Heriot-Watt University and landscape architecture at Edinburgh University, he practised landscape architecture with Colvin & Moggridge in Oxfordshire before joining the Countryside Commission as its Landscape Architect in 1975.

Our countryside landscapes are man-made and their beauty or lack of beauty is largely the result of man's influence. Buildings are an integral part of these landscapes and again man's influence will determine whether their contribution enhances or mars the beauty of the landscape (7.1). At the end of the day we are concerned with the influence of the landowner or manager on countryside landscapes. I should like to look at this influence with reference to areas where the proportion of buildings to more natural elements is low, our farmed landscapes; and to areas where the proportion of buildings to natural elements is high, the urban fringe, in order to determine what effect man's influence is having on these landscapes; I then want to compare this effect with what the general public expect of countryside and how they would like to use it and finally to discuss ways in which the public's expectation and the landowners reality can be made compatible.

7.1
The village and church of Clun, Shropshire
The harmonious and complementary relationship of buildings and landscape in the countryside.

Changing farm landscapes

The Countryside Commission's New Agricultural Landscapes study of 1972 was set up to determine the impact of modern farming methods on English lowland landscapes. The study's findings strongly indicated that many of the lowland landscapes inherited from earlier generations had been, or soon would be, replaced by new landscapes of greatly diminished scenic and wildlife value (7.2). The reason for this was that farmers in the main saw the maximisation of productivity or of profit from productivity as their sole concern. Anything which was not functional to this end was changed, destroyed or neglected. Hedges were taken out if by doing so a more efficient use of labour, mechanisation and time could be achieved. Otherwise hedges were maintained if functional and neglected if not. Ponds and wetlands were drained and small woods felled and the land put to more productive and profitable use. Woods which could not be profitably felled or managed were neglected. Water courses were straightened and dredged to improve drainage and edge vegetation and trees cleared to assist maintenance. Permanent pasture, heath and moorland was ploughed and reseeded with productive grasses. Old farm buildings were neglected and new, larger farm buildings necessary to the increased farm size, the increased productivity or herd size and to modern management and mechanisation, were erected with new mass-produced materials and with an independence of the landscape made possible by modern technology, piped water and electricity. New woods and hedgerow trees were not planted because it was not profitable to do so and their disadvantages outweighed their advantages. The consequences of these actions were a loss of variety and diversity, a loss of landscape elements, a loss of wildlife habitats and a new more open landscape in which the lack of harmony between the new farm buildings and their traditional neighbours and between the new farm buildings and the landscape was obvious.

7.2
Ely, Cambridgeshire
Telegraph poles and modern farm buildings in a modern lowland farmed landscape. Ugly accretions to a visually bare and lifeless landscape.

Utilitarian approach

These consequences were entirely logical given food production as the sole function of our farmed landscapes. Furthermore, the changes did not imply a change in attitude of farmers. Sir Kenneth Clark in

7.3
Ipsden, Oxfordshire
The traditional landscape going. In flat landscapes the removal of hedges and hedgerow trees highlights the importance of woods as vertical counterpoint and relief from the remorseless, horizontal emphasis of the new landscapes. The buildings have lost touch with their landscape and stand isolated and alone with only the old farm building being tied to the ground through its dark, low slung roof.

Landscape into art has unkindly observed that farmers 'are almost the only class of the community who are not enthusiastic about natural beauty'. Farmers actions have always been directed towards the highly functional and practical ends of food production. The enclosure landscapes which we have come to love and whose passing we now deplore were functional landscapes brought into existence through ruthless bureaucratic means. Those landscapes were also bitterly disliked and caused considerable changes in wildlife habitat. All that has changed today is the means by which farmers achieve their functional goals (7.3).

The urban fringe

In the urban fringe, meanwhile, the same utilitarian approach was being taken in a piecemeal and unrelated fashion so that the land was used for an assortment of activities which serviced the town but were inappropriate in both the town and the open countryside. Thus the urban fringe was used for hospitals and sanatoriums, prisons, airfields, slaughter houses, sewage works, sports grounds, mineral workings, water works, electricity sub-stations, reservoirs and rubbish tips. In amongst these activities was farmland whose management was considerably influenced by the surrounding land-uses. The result was again a landscape impoverished of beauty, wildlife value and recreational opportunity. Furthermore the problems engendered by this un-coordinated use of land, if identified at all, were seen in isolation, neither linked outwards to the activities and resources of the countryside nor inwards to the demands and needs of the town.

How the public see it

But, you may ask, does it matter? It obviously didn't over-concern the landowner, whether public or private, but did it matter to the general public? To answer this question the Countryside Commission conducted a number of surveys to determine the public attitude to countryside, to countryside recreation and to the urban fringe.

A comprehensive home interview was conducted for us in 1977 by the National Opinion Poll which concluded that visiting the countryside was probably one of the leading recreational activities in the country. We learned that 72% of respondents prefer the countryside as a place to spend their leisure time, while 17% prefer the town. In terms of actual behaviour, this meant that over half the population made at least one trip a month to the countryside for a day or part of a day in the summer of 1977. Significantly, 44% of trips are to places not specifically managed for recreation which emphasises the importance of multiple land-use in the management of countryside.

In further surveys, in-depth interviews and group discussions with people living in urban fringe areas and in areas progressively deeper within the hearts of our cities, we found again that over the country generally 80% of those interviewed wanted recreation in the countryside. In London, however, the number of trips actually made was less than the national average because of the difficulty, distance and cost involved, particularly for the elderly, the disabled and those without cars, of getting to what they considered countryside. On the other hand, when interviewing on a line from

Barnet back into Camden, amongst all classes and types of people, we found a considerable appreciation and use of Hampstead Heath. They said it was like countryside: that they liked it because it was uncultivated, unmanaged. They said it was better than countryside, where you never knew what you could do, as you could let children run without fear. They liked it because it was much wilder than any countryside they knew. Hampstead Heath was natural; there were no flower beds, it had ponds, open air swimming, woods and you felt close to nature. It reminded them of the way the country might have looked a hundred years ago. There was peace and quiet, by which they didn't mean the absence of people – they didn't mind them at all, but the absence of buildings, roads, mechanical noise and the sense of insecurity that these things brought. When asked about more formal parks, such as Regents Park, people found them nice but not enough. There was not the same release from urban pressures in these parks and their controlled formality and geometry was more a pale reflection of the formality and geometry of the surrounding streets and buildings than a contrast to them. The feeling was not of being close to nature but rather of being close to the city.

New roles for urban parks

These findings suggest that perhaps we should reassess our urban parks and urban open spaces to see if they continue to meet the needs of people and whether we shouldn't, where appropriate in some cases, introduce a wilder, more natural and less managed feeling with structural diversity and plant variety which will both encourage wildlife and stimulate imagination; introduce not just trees but countryside into our towns and cities.

Emotional attachment

Taken more broadly these findings do suggest that the countryside of the urban fringe and of our farm landscapes, do have a recreational role to play, and further that our concept of countryside is complex. It's much more than a simple definition of land-use, of the predominance of natural systems or of the lack of buildings. We have a deep and emotional attachment to an idea of countryside. Additionally, in a world, particularly an urban world where we are subjected to so much change and have to constantly adapt to increasing technological innovation, we tend to look to countryside to sustain that important belief in the unchangeability, the constancy of certain aspects of our lives. The countryside is seen as a complex, subtle and intimate blend of rural interests and functions, of vegetational variety and structural diversity, of vista and enclosure, of natural beauty and wildlife, of woods and streams, of rich earthy smells after rain, of colour and fast moving cloud shadow, of the sound of wind and of wild creatures, of the contact with natural things. Countryside gives us a sense of continuity. It reminds us of our roots, of our place in nature and dependence on nature. It is the background and framework for our lives. It really is no good saying that this view is totally unrealistic, that in fact the countryside is the farmer's factory floor or a servicing area for the town. To be sure, this level of expectation needs to be tempered through an understanding of how a countryside works and of the need for change, but it cannot be ignored, it must inform what we do in the countryside. Town and country are interdependent and the countryside can properly be regarded as a majority interest. The landowners limited functional use of land, when looked at in this way, can be seen to be a sub-optimum solution; a solution which is right when considered within the narrow parameters from which it arises, but wrong when seen in the light of this much broader concept of the function of countryside. Somehow a compromise must be found.

Multiple land-use and area management

The Countryside Commission sees multiple landuse and co-ordinated management measures applied on an area basis as the means of reconciling conflicting uses and ideals in the interests of an accessible and, in its broader definition, functional countryside; a countryside of beauty and wildlife. Through a number of projects we are showing that this approach is practical.

Demonstration farms

We are setting up twelve demonstration farms to test our belief that multiple landuse is still a practical option for farmers. The farms will be representative of the main farming types and landscapes in England and Wales and will be established with the following broad objectives:

1. To assess the feasibility of preparing and implementing management plans, which balance the needs of commercial farming with those of conservation without significantly reducing farm productivity;

2. To compare the different methods by which compromise plans are implemented on the farm;

3. To carefully monitor the physical, financial and managerial changes involved; and

4. To demonstrate to the farming community and those concerned with conservation the results achieved.

All are to be working farms of typical size and management for their area and both owners and tenants will need to be aware of, if not committed to, the need for landscape and wildlife conservation. To date we have set up nine of the twelve proposed farms. It takes up to three years to prepare and fully implement a multi-purpose farm plan, but we are convinced that this project will make a unique contribution to our case that you do not have to have a countryside impoverished of wildlife and beauty in order to farm efficiently. The first of the farms will be available for demonstration this year, but reasonably visits will be restricted by invitation or appointment.

Work on these farms, together with the results of the studies carried out by us on a range of problems including the future of small woods, the conservation of traditional farm buildings, the design and siting of modern farm buildings and management agreements, will be used to produce a definitive series of practical advisory leaflets. The Forestry Commission and the Nature Conservancy Council will also be contributing their expertise to what will be known collectively as the *Countryside Conservation Handbook*. The project is jointly sponsored by the National Farmers Union and the Country Landowners Association, and the leaflets will be available free from them, but additionally we hope to get copies into the hands of all farmers through the use of ADAS officers. The handbook will be launched this year.

New Agricultural Landscapes

Looking further than the individual farm and at area management, we have been setting up what we term New Agricultural Landscape projects. The methodology used in these projects was initially tested in the uplands and found to work. The approach consists of appointing a project officer, attached to the local authority and with a background in agriculture — this is important if he or she is to gain the confidence of farmers — to liaise with farmers, landowners and local interest groups and gain their co-operation in bringing about management action aimed at promoting landscape and wildlife conservation and enhancement (7.4).

Beginning in an initial area of about 5000 hectares, but expanding later if successful, the project officer will first identify existing landscape and wildlife features of particular importance. He will then have the task of persuading those responsible for land management, both farmers and public authorities, to maintain these features and to undertake both new planting and the creation of wildlife habitats. An important aspect of the project officer's role will be giving advice and arranging the carrying out of conservation work with whatever resources are available and practical, including voluntary labour and of promoting the various grants available for tree planting, management work and conservation generally. In addition to existing grants the project officer will have a special budget at his disposal — whose spending will be free of red tape controls — to carry out desirable work not covered by current grant

7.4
The Barton Hills near Barton-le-Clay, Bedfordshire
Also the traditional landscape. In such rolling country the removal of hedgerows and their trees allows the land's flowing beauty to be expressed without constraint. Woods give dark contrast and act as islands of visual stability in such restlessly moving landform.

aid schemes. In the countryside we find a little money goes a very long way. The key word in these exercises is flexibility so that the project officer can act quickly and take full advantage of any opportunity presented to him or her for implementing landscape and wildlife conservation measures.

The Commission sees the end product of these projects as not only the conservation works that the project officer initiates, but also what he or she can achieve by sowing the seed of conservation in the minds of farmers and landowners through example, advice, making a convincing case for conservation and through demonstrating practically that conservation is compatible with modern farming. Project officers for the first two agricultural landscape projects in Hereford & Worcester and in Suffolk, were appointed in June of

7.5
Sewage works, Bollin Valley, Manchester
The urban fringe as the location for an unrelated assortment of activities which serve the town but which are inappropriate in both the town and the open countryside.

1978 and work is now underway. A number of other county councils have expressed interest and we are now negotiating similar projects with them.

Urban fringe

This same approach to area management involving the use of the project officer as a catalyst has been successfully tried out in urban fringe areas such as the Bollin Valley in the Manchester urban fringe (7.5) and in the London urban fringe at Havering and at Hertfordshire/Barnet. Following on from these urban fringe experiments the Commission now intends a major urban fringe experiment involving the whole urban fringe of a major industrial town or city of some one quarter to a half million inhabitants and will cover up to 200 square miles. This five year experiment will involve the Commission in sponsoring and helping to pay for work which:

1. Enables the land around the chosen centre to be farmed more productively and efficiently;

2. Improves relations between visitors from the urban area and local people concerned with farming, forestry and water conservation;

3. Clears eyesores, including derelict land and buildings, and controls pollution;

4. Improves the state of footpaths, bridleways, water areas, public open spaces, small car parks, picnic sites and country parks, and provides new amenities where necessary;

5. Provides more and better small amenity woodlands, trees and shrubs and helps to maintain good quality landscape features such as hedgerows, field walls and minor buildings;

6. Increases care for wildlife habitats; and

7. Gives local residents and visitors better opportunities to understand, appreciate and enjoy the countryside around them.

The project is scheduled to commence in 1980 and its cost could amount to several million pounds.

Tree-planting in Norfolk

An important element in this comprehensive approach to area management is the local authority amenity tree planting schemes which the Commission promotes and grant aids. The Commission's expenditure on amenity tree planting has risen from £123,000, three years ago to an estimated £1,200,000 this financial year, but we are aware that there is a very real danger that the landscapes resulting from many of these planting efforts will appear fragmented and lack cohesion. A reason for this is that the initiative for planting usually rests with the farmers who then approach their local authorities and because the farmer's preference for planting sites and often choice of species too, is usually accepted. As a result there is often a lack of visual co-ordination between holdings. For this reason Norfolk County Council's tree planting scheme is worth consideration since it promotes an approach which could largely overcome this problem.

Each year an area of the county is selected for an intensive tree planting campaign; the choice of area being based on the quality of the existing tree cover. Having defined the area, aerial photographs and maps are obtained which when used in conjunction with a ground survey give an overall impression of the landscape and allow the county to identify the essential characteristics of the existing tree cover. This information is used later in the design of the new planting. A land ownership map is then drawn up with the help of the farmers and information given to the farmers on the scheme — its objectives, finance and implementation. A general picture of the farming community is built up; the response of the farmers noted and potential planting sites identified. The County is thus giving itself the opportunity to create a cohesive landscape effect. When sites have been agreed with each farmer the County draws up plans, organises the planting contract, purchases the trees and carries out the administration associated with the Countryside Commission's grant aid. The landowner's involvement is limited to approving sites and paying a proportion of the scheme. This is a great incentive to the farmers who would otherwise be too busy and lack the expertise to organise their own planting schemes. The work is then carried out under a single contract and schemes may therefore be included that would normally be too small for grant aid. Norfolk County Council is to be congratulated also for embarking upon a twenty five year programme for the restoration of the Norfolk landscape, involving, in order to reverse the decline in the numbers of farmland trees, an annual planting target of 80,000 trees.

Changing attitudes

Much of this Commission work has arisen out of our New Agricultural Landscapes policy, which calls for a series of measures aimed at reversing the landscape decline taking place on both publicly and privately owned land. This policy also calls for a change of attitude since, although we can show that multiple landuse and a comprehensive approach to land management works, we will not see the approach adopted by both private and public landowners until they care sufficiently about the objectives which these approaches set out to achieve. We believe progress is best achieved through the active co-operation of those directly concerned, whether landowners or local authorities, companies or communities. We have had some very good responses.

The Forestry Commission has reintroduced the small woods scheme and now actively take landscape, wildlife and recreation into account in the design and management of their forests. The National Farmers Union and the Country Landowners Association have produced a code of practice for private owners and occupiers of land entitled *Caring for the countryside* which calls on farmers and landowners to take positive action to conserve landscape and wildlife and is a very significant step forward. The Ministry of Agriculture is showing signs of taking an active interest in the landscape, wildlife and recreational implications of farming and have been encouraged to do so further by a recently published Strutt Report. However, we have a long way to go before individual landowners and managers accept and manage for this wider concept of the function of countryside.

8 A countryman's view

John Weller

John Weller, RIBA, is a member of the councils of Men of Trees and Land, and of the executive council of the Professional Institutions Council for Conservation. He lives in Bildeston, Suffolk, and practises architecture with special reference to the design of farm buildings, on which his book *Farm buildings: Structural techniques and materials*, is a standard work. He also lectures at the Chelmer Institute's Department of Planning.

Many years ago I spent seven years training to be an architect, at the end of which time I was brainwashed to the extent that I loved my deciduous woodlands, full of incipient decay, because they gave romance of colour, shape and variety. It was then perhaps my good fortune later to spend another year amongst agricultural economists at Cambridge. At the end of that time I gained a different perspective as to what the aesthetics of landscape could be about. I saw in the coordinated conifers, aspects of visual delight because they represented a delight of control over nature, order of management and efficiency of profit. I think it is very important to understand this apparent dichotomy in the appreciation of what delight is about.

Trees as a crop

We love variety — we love disorder, but those farmers who manage land and manage it well to produce food, crops or other commodities, have what I think is equally an aesthetic which gives them pleasure. If we deny them that aesthetic I think we do ourselves and them a disservice.

I want in relation to that to consider trees in the countryside as a crop, as part of our historic landscape and then in relation to the microscale. We produce from our own shores only eight per cent of our consumption of timber. Ninety two per cent is imported at a very great cost of several thousand million pounds a year, and the reason for this is that we have gainsaid over the last fifty years the wisdom of the Forestry Commission who have been raring to go to plant more, so that succeeding generations might reap that crop. But because it is implicit in our understanding that there is no aesthetic beauty in the conifers, there has been public pressure against afforestation. However, it has been clearly shown by Dame Sylvia Crowe and now by Clifford Tandy, as consultants to the Forestry Commission, that large landscapes can indeed absorb bold planting schemes if there is some understanding of contour and colour.

A revival of coppicing?

I believe very firmly that, whereas we have ignored our grandfathers and our fathers, if we are wise today we plant for our grandchildren and during the 1980's we should see to it that another two million hectares go under afforestation. So that in another fifty to sixty years' time those that succeed us will begin to reap the benefit.

The second thing which I think is very much misunderstood and particularly by an urban public, is that historically trees were coppiced as a rotational crop and this was done to provide many different uses, for craft tools, for wattle and fuel. And indeed if you look at the landscape you will see the remnants of the pollards there which was a symbol of a well-structured rural economy, which was indeed destroyed by our fathers. I think that we must begin to rethink trees not only as an aesthetic, which they are, but as a crop which can enrich our lives in many different ways (8.1).

8.1
Groton Wood Coppice, Suffolk
Ancient coppice woodland showing massive standards, now rare, from very old stools — now being remanaged by the Suffolk Trust for Nature Conservation.

Those of you who perhaps live in the countryside like I do and take the rural magazines as I do, *The Countryman, Country Landowner, Farmers Weekly* and the others, when you turn to the back pages you will find them absolutely riddled with adverts for wood-burning stoves. There is a great belief that they are of benefit and are cheap to run, which is partially true.

At present they are mainly using the decaying elms of our countryside but God willing, that will be of short duration, and what I look to is that we should begin again to coppice our trees, and as I see it every village should form a wood-burning stove society. I don't think it is likely to be economic for farmers to grow trees here and there in odd corners, on wasteland, and to coppice them because the labour costs will rule it out of court. I see it as quite practical for a farmer to grow trees for coppicing which he will then let to a local society who would manage them on a lease and would coppice them and would provide the fuel for the stoves that are now going into our cottages. And on this basis once again we will have trees in our countryside not just because we like them there to look at but because they are contributing to a mixed rural economy.

Historic landscapes

I want to talk also of our historic landscape. Near where I live in Suffolk is the Great Wood of Bradfield, which a farmer wanted to erase in order to increase his productivity – a very understandable objective. The planners, bless their hearts, were going to aid and abet him but a small local pressure group said no, we like those trees, we like that wood, and when the historians moved in they found to our great interest and delight that it was one of the few remaining woods managed by one of the greatest abbeys of Europe, that of Bury St. Edmunds, and there was clear evidence in that wood of how it had been coppiced and managed over 800 years, on a rotational basis. But I think, and again a great deal of thought has to go into this as we do not even have much knowledge, that we need to look at the countryside as an evolving historic fabric. Hoskins apart, there are few that have dedicated their lives to this task.

Beware historic sites

We also need to think a little bit about where we plant trees in relation to historic landscapes. The Countryside Commission, as Paul Walshe tells us in Chapter 7, are – quite rightly – keen that we should plant trees in the countryside – preferably not in a fragmented way but with some thought as to the landscape and contour qualities. The Tree Council too, bless their hearts, support this same vision of more trees in the landscape, and yet I am concerned – there seems to be very little coordination behind the scenes, that all this tree planting which is being encouraged should not cover that very exceptional and rare Roman temple site. We need to think in terms of the historic fabric that lies beneath the soil as well as above it, before we allow development and change.

Trees, hedges, and buildings

I want to give one or two particulars on the relationship of trees and hedges to the smaller scale environment. When we plant trees or seek for trees, in the countryside, we are often relating them to contours and buildings over a distance of a mile or two miles in order to get the rapport that we seek. It is not a question necessarily of trees having to be close to buildings and their foundations in order to get a relationship. You will be aware, and the Ministry of Agriculture, bless them, have put it about that whereas – in the past, ignorant as they were, they gave grants to grubbing out hedges – they have now learnt the error of their ways and have stopped that. It is true, they now call them ditching grants. And this is a fact – if you have a ditch and grub it out and clear it for better drainage, and if there is a hedge in the way you will get a grant for cleaning out the ditch – you will also get a grant for removing the hedge so you can clean out the ditch. It's a little bit unfair perhaps but I know of several cases near me where hedges have disappeared with grant aid on that basis (8.2, 8.3).

Shelter-belts and hedgerow profiles

When we put shelter belts in the countryside, which I believe we should, within permanent grassland as in the past, then they can be those great wide swathes of trees going over hill and over dale, which look so attractive in Yorkshire and other parts. But where you place

8.2 and 8.3
Willows, before and after
Trees, important as they are to the composition of the landscapes, are a nuisance to some people. These were destroyed by the Water Authority so that a dredger could work from the road.

shelter belts in relation to planted crops, be they grass or cabbages or corn, then they should be filigree, above a low bush fuzz. Not to stop the wind but to reduce its speed, and therefore perhaps not quite as attractive as these great wadges of desiduous trees which we mostly think of when we talk about shelter belts.

Secondly, when we have hedgerows (and they're very questionable in terms of food production) they should be of a shape to provide wildlife with the diversity of habitat which gives it balance. A great deal of thought is going ahead as to how we can maintain these types of shaped hedges. New types of cultivation equipment are under investigation and it does look as though in a year or two we'll have fairly simple tools which can trim those hedges, perhaps on an annual basis. And though in many places we still see a landscape full of hedges, when you look at them closely they are often in a period of decay and decline. They're weak at their knees. Learning how to manage, look after, keep and to rotate hedges is something that we need to think about.

Farm buildings and trees

Buildings need to be sited with very particular care — especially farm buildings in relation to trees and hedges, since stock and crop enclosures which are what we in our jargon call buildings are sensitive to balances of ventilation. There is a great deal of ignorance in the farm building world and particularly amongst those that mass manufacture buildings for farmers, as to how they react to the micro-climate. We see many cases of disaster or near-disaster, of badly ventilated buildings, which stem from our ignorance of how they relate to the down draughts and the pressures and the suctions caused by wind coming over buildings and over trees in proximity to the new building. Farm buildings, particularly stock buildings, are either semi-open, semi-controlled environments or totally controlled environments and each has its own particular problems of micro-climate that vegetation can bring (8.4).

Paying for landscape conservation?

We have in farm country, something called the Field Monuments Scheme whereby the farmer is given a pitiful grant not to erase some field monument, but which is so derisory a sum that very few have applied to take up the scheme. But there is implied in that, and implied in the kind of talk I hear at all the rural conferences I go to, a growing and affirming belief that if farmers are denied taking out a hedge or cutting down a tree, erasing a field monument or knocking down an old farm building because it restricts as it does their profitable development of their farm, they should thereby be granted compensation. Conference after conference I go to says quite clearly — and the CPRE too tends to support this — that if we want a nice looking landscape with its historic features, and the trees and hedges retained, then we must be prepared to put cash on the table.

8.4
Warren Farm, Lambourne, Berkshire
A complex for 200 calves and 600 head of beef cattle, together with all the necessary feed and ancilliary buildings. Good grouping within the folds of downland. Trees are vital to composition, but they do not have to be among the buildings — the overall landscape is the composition which the eye appreciates.

An anomalous difference

I go along with this to a large extent, but what does worry me is this — and it niggles in my mind when I go into a building like the RIBA in Portland Place, which is rather inefficient for modern needs. That building, thankfully, is listed, and if ever the RIBA wanted to pull it down and redevelop the site efficiently (which they would do over my dead body), there would be a number of difficulties to overcome. There is no question, unfortunately, of the RIBA being given a nice cash grant for loss of development rights — no compensation for any owner who has taken on or inherited a listed building, a part of our 'heritage'. In the farm landscape people are coming to expect

8 A countryman's view: Weller

compensation if they forego efficiency so as to conserve the heritage. The difference is anomalous — but arguably such compensation may be a better way of doing things (8.5).

8.5
CEGB substation, Bramley
Some structures within rural areas are so uncouth in their overall mass and detail that tree screening is the only solution.

9 The green people; a Dutch view

Jan Guldemond

Ir. Jan L. Guldemond has been Director of the municipal Parks and Recreation Service in Haarlem in the Netherlands since 1973. Educated at Wageningen Agricultural University, he gained a doctorate in forestry in 1963, and from 1964 to 1973 was a research officer at the Forest Research Institute, Wageningen, specialising in the problems of trees in urban areas. He is Chairman of the Dutch Association of Directors of Parks and Recreation.

Let me first introduce myself. I am the director of the municipal service of parks, forests, gardens and cemeteries of Haarlem in Holland. I prefer to call it 'urban green service'. You will understand that the word 'green' in this context means more than grass alone, namely all the horizontal and vertical green. In our service, 250 men are working for the green of a town of 175,000 inhabitants in the coastal area near the North Sea. Formerly I was a research officer at the Forest Research Institute in Wageningen, where I worked mainly with deciduous trees. So am I, it may be asked, the most qualified man to write about urban trees or city woodlands, when in the field of landscaping here in your country are so many famous names and traditions? Am I a man with striking or even revolutionary inventions? Or do I have ready-to-hand recipes for you? I don't believe it. I am just a representative of a lot of green people in our country, concerned with the problem of how to establish and to keep a green environment under the conditions of today and in agreement with natural, ecological principles. We have developed some — in my eyes rather simple — techniques in that direction: I will tell you about our philosophy and maybe you can use some of my words as building bricks for your own thoughts.

Ecological equilibrium destroyed

Once upon a time there was a situation in our country in which you could characterize the environment with 'stability, equilibrium, harmony and rest'. The land and its use by inhabitants were more or less in balance. In the use of the ground in our country, the woodlands and other plantations did not play a dominating role, it is true, and the forest area was modest (a few per cent of the total land) and was heterogeneous in quality and spreading. The vertical green of trees and shrubs belonged still as a matter of course to the horizontal green of meadows and fields and the pattern of the farms, villages, little towns, waters and dykes. There was a kind of organic growth in the landscape. The atmosphere was peaceful and quiet and there was plenty of room. In such a situation, little need is felt to increase very much the planting of trees and shrubs. When the equilibrium was broken, with a rapid increase in population,

The green people; a Dutch view: Guldemond

explosively developing building and industrialisation, harmful pollution of the environment, intensively growing traffic and vanishing distances, then the role of the green areas becomes more and more important in the pattern of life of the regions in danger.

Creating green zones

A movement began from the traditional and not very important production forests on poor soils and the almost 'automatically' grown landscape elements towards pure amenity and recreation forests on richer soils and finally towards urban greenbelts and even green zones in the cities on all types of soils, also artificial ones. When you look at all kinds of plans for development in our country, you see that everywhere much attention has been paid to the achievement of large green areas. These green areas are zones of forests, recreational provisions and water, which are in the dense populated and built over parts of our land not only the green carpets between grey living blocks where man can relax, but which have also other functions (9.1). In fact we try to make them as multi-functional as possible: for protection against climatological influences, for the battle against pollution, for production of wood (don't forget that please!), as important landscape elements and as places to live in.

9.1
Four years old plantation in a green wedge between living blocks.

Unfavourable habitats

This was a new stage indeed. Previously changes had been small and there were always experiences and knowledge from the past to rely on. Now new plantations must be carried out on soil types and under circumstances of which we had little experience and knowledge, particularly in urban regions. I do not only mean better, richer soil types but also peculiar types: grounds raised by spouting sand, clay, peat or mixtures; grounds covered with refuse dumps; soil types with a high groundwater table and a therefore weak structure and so on. Moreover there were unfavourable climatological conditions (think of the wind in the coastal area, where most people live and the need for new plantations is the greatest!) and other limiting factors as pollution, salt, influences from living, working, building and traffic, the cutting up into small parts by roads for instance. On one hand we finally got the opportunity to play a new role; on the other hand, with our lack of experience in this new environment we had to be careful to avoid blunders, which would demand more time and money. Therefore we mobilized all possible research institutes and management services to tackle the problems. In close co-operation a lot of work has been done in experimental plantations, in observation plots, in soil survey and mapping out. It is now possible to predict the results of new plantations under different circumstances, provided that planting is adjusted carefully to differing circumstances. When I say 'adjust' the planting, I mean look at the soil, the climate, the prevailing circumstances, the final purpose of the plantation, and then make a choice of species, system of establishment and so on. Not the other way round by trying to adjust the circumstances to the once chosen plantation system.

Ecological solecisms

Weed control and fertilisation for instance are valuable help during the establishment period, but not destined to keep in life a plantation not suitable to the growing site. You should use specific species and establishment systems for specific growing sites. It is therefore wrong to use blindly a 'standard assortment' in all circumstances. First of all a thorough research of the growing site must be done, including a soil classification and an evaluation of the suitability for the various plantation types. A sound knowledge of the possible different soil types is the only good starting point for new plantations to make the right choice. Don't forget that the establishment of plantations for forestry or amenity purposes is a kind of soil use, which in itself is not different from agriculture or horticulture. Also with plantations you establish a relation between vegetation and site, where the vegetation (the crop in agriculture and horticulture) must be able to thrive. It is normal in the agriculture *not* to use wheat on drift-sand or sugarbeet on peat-bog or asparagus on heavy clay, why do I see then so often strange things in plantations, especially those with an amenity or landscape purpose? Poplars in dry sand, beeches on wet peat and conifers on heavy clay, just to mention a few things, are as absurd as the agricultural example. Oh yes, of course, you don't want a crop, you are not aiming at production. But in amenity planting, too, you should obey the laws of nature, the demands which the different species have; in short: you should aim at an ecological justified use of the site.

Plant before you build

This is, of course, easier to fulfil in large areas, where you can work on a large scale, than on the small scale which is often forced upon you near — let alone in — the cities. That is true, but also when you miss the advantage of the large scale forestablishment and management in phases, you have the obligation to work according to natural principles, even on the smallest scale, when you are planting just one tree on a city square. The smaller plantations in the direct influence of the urban surrounding are as necessary and important as the large recreation areas far away. Therefore, whether we work in the vast polders or in the city greenbelts or in green wedges inside the cities, we use the same technique. I would say, we need this technique even more in the direct influence of the cities (9.2, 9.3). In densely populated and quickly urbanizing regions, especially there where the need of quick growing healthy green is the greatest, it is important to have an active and progressive green policy, based upon undeniable natural laws. It is practically impossible to have enough green of older age and sufficient mass ready for every new

9.2
Aerial view on a green edge around a new city district, six years old.

9.3
The same spot as illustration 9.2. Plantation quite close to the buildings.

Painting with an axe

concentration of people in a just built quarter, however desirable that may be. All the more important, then, that we take measure in good time to guarantee at least enough young green elements at the time when people are occupying the new quarter. If at all possible planting should start before building operations — the earlier the better. In this way planting can get a head-start on people, can grow up closely and improve the environment beforehand. By using fast-growing pioneers you soon get results for the future inhabitants and assist management (think of micro-climate, continuity, durability, and flexibility).

Alas the situation is often so that the green people do not work beforehand, but afterwards like a green paper-hanger, when the building is entirely finished. That cannot be a real green policy. Real green policy starts early, when all building projects are still on the drawing boards, in close co-operation between town and green planners and builders. In this respect green people ought to be leaders, not followers, because otherwise the final situation can easily get a structure unfavourable for good plantations and therefore for the environment of the people. And also in this respect I cannot agree with all those large open spaces, just lying there and waiting for the future. Notwithstanding all objections and troubles, these spaces should be planted as soon as possible, if need be with a temporary plantation. The final landscaping can come afterwards: then you can landscape in a plantation that exists already, which is an easier way of working. Painting with an axe, we call that.

'Prairie planting' in Britain

The challenge for the green people is not to miss any opportunities. Lost opportunities mean defects in the environment, places used for other purposes, or even spaces that are too open — where, with more forethought, quick-wittedness and expertise, there could have been tree planting. I am sorry to say this, but in your country too, there are examples of plenty of space, yes the nearly 'holy' open space, where almost nothing breaks the vast levels of grass, concrete and asphalt, or separates them with sufficient vertical green. There are young trees yes, but they are planted so wide, that they will have their right space after a century. There is not any pioneer generation of plants, which could give pleasure *now* and which would be the first step to a dynamic development and a climax-stage. It is as if the whole has been seen as static and with the model of an old park in mind all young trees have been planted in the arrangement and on the distance of old ones. Shrubs are often totally absent, and we have had almost aggressive lines of buildings and roads in the picture. Nowhere is there any softening of the industry or the traffic, nor is there any influence on the microclimate, for instance protection against wind. Inhabitants walk and sit on open places, benches have no shelter, playgrounds lie in open grass plains without any protection or separation by shrubs. The human scale is lost, which does not matter everywhere, but is bad in a living environment.

Mixture of ages needed

9.4
A forest landscape between the city buildings. Use of pioneer species (poplar), eight years old.

To establish the city woodlands and to seize every opportunity is the first task. The second, as important as the first, is to maintain them! Only continuous care can guarantee permanence. This care means efficient arboricultural attention and management measures during the whole life. It also means thinning, cutting and replanting in time, no matter if these activities are pleasant (popular) or not. We are never finished with our job, plantations should never reach the absolute end. There must be continuation, also with very old trees. Old trees are valuable and beautiful and their conservation, where it is possible and justified, is a good thing (9.4). No manager however, can be congratulated when a forest or park or collection of street trees is only a mausoleum of old, weak trees with defects, while no young trees give a prospect for a future without large gaps. He who just saves old trees and does not bother himself about the planting of young ones to take over some time, goes to meet the day when there is nothing left. When you want old tree stands to be maintained 'eternally' they should be rejuvenated and in time! This applies to the forest, the large park, the small public garden, yes even to the street. We must plant for our grandchildren's pleasure. They will want to see old trees, so we will have to plant them. That means we cannot just wait and let the old tree stands die out. We have to respect natural principles which imply a normal distribution of ages. Quite a responsibility isn't it? And that is why I always have a rather uncomfortable feeling when I see once more a park or an estate full of wonderful old trees, splendid to look at, but without any young material for the future and so without the permanence we all wish. I am a forester by origin, and I know where that leads – to dreary decay. You can see it everywhere – in my country, in yours too, all over Europe: parks which resemble homes for old people. When a calamity occurs, a storm, a period of drought, an elm disease, then you see the weakness and vulnerability of an over-aged stand without rejuvenation. Don't misunderstand me. I like to see old people and hope that they live as long as possible, but I want to see them together with children, with middle-aged people, with all ages in one society, regularly composed.

Six principles for planting

The time factor plays an important, in fact a decisive role in all our work, including with plantations: timely planning, early time of planting, dividing the life of a plantation into time phases, time of thinning, cutting and rejuvenating. Add to this the fact that in urban regions the development is very rapid. Plantations should have a quick pace and in fact they should be ready and full-grown 'tomorrow' if you listen to the wishes of the people. It is therefore, clear that we cannot take the risk of delay or even failure. We will have to play safe and that means always a way according to the demands of nature.

Finally, I would put forward the following propositions:

1. The plantation of city woodlands must be planned in time in teamwork with town and country planners, designers and builders and should be ready before the building phase is ended.

2. City woodlands should give quick results, therefore an initial use of quick growing species is desirable.

3. For plantations on soil types which are planted for the first time a considerable use of pioneer species is necessary, especially under extreme climatic conditions.

4. The establishment of plantations must be ecological and arboriculturally justified. This means among other things choosing species which can grow healthily on a site during their whole life.

5. All functions of woodlands amenity, recreation, landscaping, production, protection and so on benefit from healthy growing, vital plantations with normal management, not establishment with species which can only be kept alive 'by hook and crook' at very high costs.

6. To reach permanence it is necessary to keep a plantation always under control and to aim at rejuvenation from the beginning.

Search for new techniques

After this 'creed', I should like to add the following: 'There appears to be a need for an intense effort to raise the general level of amenity tree management practices. We have a superb history of arboricultural achievement in Britain, but the rapidly changing social and physical environment calls for the development of new techniques and attitudes in amenity tree management'. These two sentences are not mine of course; I am not quite that self-opinionated. I simply quote from the report of the British Arboricultural Research Working Party of 1973. I hope this chapter contributes a little to those objectives. There is an old Dutch proverb which may perhaps appeal to your sea-faring nation, even when discussing city woodlands: 'When the tide turns, change your tack!' (9.5).

9.5
It is so easy to have a nice environment in a short time. This plantation is eight years old and situated in the immediate vicinity of a nine storey high building.

10 Trees in the inner city

Ian White

Ian White, FILA, runs a small practice in Glasgow which has been involved with urban renewal landscape work for the past five years. Consultant to the City of Glasgow District Council, the Scottish Development Agency and the Scottish Special Housing Association. Current projects include: Urban gap sites in Glasgow; parks in Glasgow; Port Glasgow; Paisley Stornoway; housing landscape in Glasgow and a Country Park at Loch Lomond.

From the safety, security and smugness of suburbia it is tempting to believe that 'environmental improvement schemes' can solve the problems of inner city areas. Some people believe that by dispensing trees with benevolence and largesse amongst the multiply-deprived in their multiply-deprived areas guarantees that all will be well — provided, of course, that the trees are not vandalised by the ungrateful recipients. I am astounded at such a view because it represents on the one hand, extreme faith or optimism, and on the other a serious lack of understanding of the real benefits which can be achieved by tree planting in inner city areas. Evidence of the failure of this approach abounds; where well-meant but ill-conceived improvements lie un-used, un-managed, and by their shoddy, neglected appearance contribute more to continuing decline than gradual improvement.

People need convincing it will work

I suspect that there are two reasons for this sorry situation; firstly that arboriculturalists, landscape architects and similar persons, although themselves dedicated and skilled, have frequently failed to convince others of the essential value of tree planting; and secondly that perhaps we have been less sensitive to the special problems of inner city areas than we imagine, therefore we continue to employ traditional methods of new and different problems instead of developing fresh and relevant approaches.

Three factors should influence our general approach to tree planting in inner city areas:

1. Realisation of the extent and complexity of inner city problems recognises the urgent need for change but also raises doubts and uncertain visions of our future urban areas. People who live and work in inner city areas need evidence to convince them that change and improvement are possible *now*. Immediate proof is required to generate the hope, enthusiasm, determination and involvement which are essential to the success of long-term strategies (10.1, 10.2).

10.1 and 10.2
Auchinlea Park, Glasgow
Before and after.

2. 'Dereliction and decay are depressing' — how often do we read or write this, but usually believing that it applies to other people, the captive urban populations who lack the resources to escape to the safety and security of suburbia. On the contrary I believe that all our futures will be largely determined by the way we tackle inner city problems and the success we achieve. Further I do not imagine that the aspirations and needs of inner city populations differ in any way from other sectors of the community, except that their expectations seem remarkably low, and are qualified by a general feeling of disbelief that 'this time something will happen'.

3. Inner city areas represent a considerable test of our ideals, knowledge, skills and relevance. We have the opportunity to demonstrate and prove that tree planting can improve the quality of life in urban areas not merely as a decorative embellishment but as part of the basic structure of urban life.

Trees can help the inner city

So if the question is asked 'Why plant trees?' then the advantages should be clearly stated:

1. Tree planting is a creative activity in direct contrast to the demolition and clearance which is characteristic of inner city areas. It achieves change and improvement in tangible terms which are of immediate benefit to the community (10.3, 10.4).

It can realise the full potential of external spaces by introducing new dimensions and perspectives; it can be a powerful and refreshing method of problem-solving provided always it is based on a sound and sympathetic understanding of *need* and *place*.

2. Tree planting is relevant throughout the entire range of spatial problems. Trees can and should be used in all types and sizes of development, and are especially relevant to the treatment of the large areas of open space which are characteristically generated in inner city areas.

3. Contrary to popular belief tree planting can achieve change and improvement in a remarkably short time. It is possible by careful choice of species size and density of planting to achieve instant landscape without resorting to plastic trees and grass. Trees even more than shrubs can transform the scale and emptiness of urban spaces and mature raw urban sites.

4. Tree planting achieves change and improvement using low-cost materials and a simple technology. It is not necessary to have vast sums of money to achieve good and lasting effects, the answer lies in

10.3 and 10.4
River Clyde walkway
Before and after.

fitting things together correctly and therefore the ingenuity and sensitivity of the tree-planter is a key skill.

5. Tree planting can provide diversity, pleasantness and identity for individuals and communities to a greater extent than many other forms of development. Identity with place and community is fundamentally important, diversity of experience enriches life and through careful site planning and tree planting these can be achieved, often at low thresholds.

6. Tree planting, however modest, can bring land into use, improve its appearance and increase the range of facilities within a community, usually at little cost and often when no other action is possible.

7. Tree planting schemes are flexible because they are versatile and adaptable to a greater extent than many other forms of development. There is no reason why we cannot be felling trees to create parks instead of waiting for them to grow. The advance structure planting found in many new towns is a good example of this approach.

8. Tree planting is an investment. The initial outlay is small, the recurring charges are low, growth is inevitable, and the eventual return could be considerable.

9. Tree planting can provide a matrix of opportunity which will improve the quality of life in the present and the future.

Relevant, essential – ubiquitous

So if the question is asked 'What can tree planting do to help solve the problems of inner city areas?' we should not hesitate to take every opportunity to convince people that tree planting is relevant, essential, and more importantly demonstrate the advantages of tree planting – every little gap and corner site counts. Not only should we clearly state both the long and short-term advantages of tree planting we must also realise the need to develop new approaches to tree planting.

We can begin by looking at the problems of inner city areas in a positive manner. Two commodities are generated, *land* and *time*, and by these two factors alone we have an opportunity to remedy structural deficiencies in inner city areas by creating new patterns in the distribution and forms of open space within which tree planting could be of considerable importance. While it appears that vacant land is generated in numerous yet relatively small sites, and while it is necessary to effect immediate change and improvement at a local level in the short term, it is of equal importance that we develop efficient systems for evaluating opportunities as they arise, to assemble land into larger packages which could achieve better long-term structural improvements.

Improving the climate

On what concepts should we base this long-term planning for trees in cities? In recent years most open space systems and therefore major tree planting have been based on recreation or movement, producing miles of linear open spaces along motorways, abandoned railway lines, derelict canals, or valley bottoms. While improvements and benefits have been gained through this approach it does not necessarily produce the optimum distribution of tree planting. For many years Swiss and German research has suggested that careful planning of the amount and distribution of tree planting in cities can improve climate by assisting air flow, reducing wind speed, regulating humidity, reducing temperature, absorbing dust particles, using carbon and producing oxygen. Such benefits are as fundamental to our health as recreation but can only be secured by careful consideration of the extent and patterns of major tree planting necessary to achieve improvements in city climates which may, of course, differ from patterns arising from considering recreational requirements only.

Attracting people back to cities

Some have argued for simply planting up every space as it becomes available with a view to adaption to a more definite use at a future time, to create 'Town forests'. I consider that in some instances this approach might be necessary, and in any event is preferable to leaving barren spaces, nevertheless it must be really considered, as a general approach, inadequate, unimaginative, frequently impracticable and potentially wasteful of valuable resources, in that it leaves so much to chance.

If it is necessary to devise new concepts on which to base major tree planting schemes it is equally important to retain a clear understanding of the purpose of tree planting in inner city areas.

Tree planting is required not only to improve the quality of life for existing populations, but more importantly in the long-term, to attract people back into cities. In fulfilling these objectives with limited resources it may be necessary to establish priorities, to vary standards of tree planting work, and to stick to them however unfair the short-term consequences may seem.

Diversity, and tension reducing

Within a structure and programme we must ensure that there is sufficient diversity of type and style of planting to truly enrich the quality of urban life. How thoroughly have we condemned Victorian park planting as being cumbersome and oppressive, glibly sneered at the cherry trees and rose beds of the municipal rustic style, replacing them with acres of immature grass and trees which are pale imitations of true English parkland style, or yard upon yard of mass shrub planting so characteristic of our later new towns; now we introduce the latest style of ecological planting to our cities which is as scruffy in appearance as it is sophisticated in concept. My main concern is that we too readily reject styles, that we are so influenced by fashion that we produce identical and often inappropriate tree planting schemes. Diversity should exist, and it can be achieved by relating the style and form of planting to its setting, purpose, and the expectations of the public which should not be the least consideration.

Life in inner city areas, because of its hardships produces tensions and aggression which in the long-term must be reduced. Instinctively, and with some justification, we may feel that tree planting could help towards this, yet curiously many recent tree planting schemes try to combat aggression and tension by being simple and robust, therefore by their nature frequently invite challenge or more frequently by their austerity achieve no recognition. In such circumstances I would argue for a more fragile, cherished and obvious form of tree planting than has been the recent fashion, which accepts a degree of 'wear and tear' and which is backed by an efficient and flexible management programme (10.5, 10.6).

10.5 and 10.6
Housing at Hamilton Hill, Glasgow
Before and after.

An index of 'quality of life'

While we cannot expect to have clear visions of our urban futures we cannot evade the responsibilities of devising strategies, establishing programmes of action, experimenting with styles of planting, and if these appear too great then at the very least, each one of us involved in tree planting can ensure that the results are properly and honestly monitored; as students by taking time to observe real spaces being used by real people, as academics by carrying out continuous research on current problems and solutions, and as practising designers by taking time to re-visit completed schemes to honestly evaluate their usefulness and not blaming all failures on mis-management or vandalism.

10.7
Structure planting, Inner Ring Road, Glasgow.

I do not intend to promote tree planting as the sole means of creating new city environments but merely to suggest that there are fundamental advantages to be gained, provided that we argue and demonstrate its relevance to the special problems of inner city areas (10.7). Our solutions may be simple but they can be effective.

Trees always have been an indicator of the quality of life, expressed and confirmed in country estates and suburban gardens but in today's inner city areas trees should exist not as the final seal of success, but as living and growing evidence of our aspirations and standards for the future (10.8).

10.8
Structure planting and stream improvement in advance of housing development, Warrington.

Glossary

Some technical and semi-technical terms explained

ADAS	Ministry of Agriculture's farm advisory service (Agricultural Development Advisory Service).
Colloid	Very finely particled material which will remain in suspension in liquids for long periods.
Oedometer	Instrument for measuring moisture in matter.
Heave	An upward movement of the soil's surface caused by swelling of the materials below.
Random walk	Growth (of roots) in any direction, obeying laws of chance.
Rooted volume	Volume of soil in which roots are present.
Self-mulching	Process by which surface soil layer dries and thus reduces evaporation from deeper soil below.
Shear failure	Fracture in structure of a building caused by subsidence of supporting soil.
Soil moisture deficit	In the accounting method for soil moisture, the amount of water evaporated or absorbed by plants from the water held in the soil after it has been thoroughly wetted and allowed to drain.
Sollute	A material dissolved in a liquid.
Volunteer trees	Trees which spring up unaided (or not intentionally aided) by man.

Bibliography

Achers, C. P.
Practical British Forestry
Oxford University Press

Arboricultural Association
Tree planting and preservation – the part of the planner
Conference papers 1975

Bean, W. J.
Trees and shrubs today in the British Isles
(several volumes)
John Murray, 1970

Caborn, J. M.
Shelter belts and windbreaks
Faber and Faber, 1965

Caborn, J. M.
Shelter belts and microclimates
HMSO, 1957

Carter, G.
Trees and shrubs of the British Isles
Cambridge University Press

Cherwell District Council
Grants for amenity tree planting
1978

Colvin, B.
Trees for town and country
Lund Humphries, 1972

Colvin, B.
Land and landscape
John Murray, 1970

Countryside Commission
New agricultural landscapes
1974

Countryside Commission
New agricultural landscapes: issues, objectives and actions
1976

Countryside Commission
Urban fringe
Countryside Recreation Review, Volume 1
1976

Countryside Commission
Grants for amenity tree planting and management
1977

DART
Small woodlands on farms
Countryside Commission
1979

Department of the Environment
Housing Development Notes II: Landscape of new housing
HMSO, 1973-4

Department of the Environment, Property Services Agency
Design with trees
HMSO, 1974

Essex County Council
Trees in Essex:
No. 1 The landscape
No. 2 Farmland planting
No. 3 Development sites
1974

Fairbrother, Nan
New lives, new landscapes
Architectural Press, 1974
(also Penguin books)

Forestry Commission
Forestry in the British Scene
1968

Lincolnshire CPRE
Trees for the farmer
1967

Bibliography

Lincolnshire CPRE
Trees in the village
1970

Ministry of Agriculture
Shelter belts for farmland
(leaflet 15)
HMSO

Nature Conservancy Council
Tree planting and wildlife conservation
(leaflet)
1974

Ramblers Association
The future of forestry
1972

Reece, R. A.
Problems of buildings on swelling/ shrinkable clays and their solutions
Brick Development Association, 1977

Registered Housebuilders Handbook, Part II

US Department of Agriculture, Forest Service
National forest landscape management: Volumes 1 and 2
1973

USDA Forest Service: Pacific Southwest Experimental Station
Landscape control points
1973

Ward, Colin
Vandalism
Architectural Press

Ward, Colin
The child in the city
Architectural Press

Weller, John
Farm buildings: Volumes 1 and 2
Crosby Lockwood Staples, 1964 and 1972

Weller, John
Modern agriculture and rural planning
Architectural Press, 1968

Weller, John
Farm wastes management
(with Dr. S. Willetts)
Crosby Lockwood Staples, 1976

Articles in periodicals

Treeless towns: Tarsem Flora
Landscape Design, February 1978, pp. 10-12

Protesters ask BSI to re-draft new tree code: Claire Glasspoole
Building Design, 12 May 1978, p. 10

Foundations on swelling/shrinkable clays, with particular reference to the problems caused by the summer of 1976: M. J. Tomlinson, R. Driscoll
Construction, September 1977, pp. 20-22

Foundation failures – who's to blame? A look at clay foundation failures (after 1976 drought): Peter Kelsey
Building, 1 April 1977, pp. 67-71

Trees in towns: a check list for sensible urban planting and after care: Peter Fothergill
The Architect, February 1977, pp. 54-58
HMSO